# Gilles Paquet

## Moderato cantabile

Toward principled governance
for Canada's immigration regime

# | Collaborative Decentred Metagovernance Series

This is the second in a series of books designed to define cumulatively the contours of collaborative metagovernance. At this time, there is still no canonical version of this paradigm: it is *en émergence*. This series intends to be one of many 'construction' sites to experiment with various dimensions of an effective and practical version of this new approach.

Metagovernance is the art of combining different forms or styles of governance – experimented with in the private, public and social sectors – to ensure effective coordination when power, resources and information are widely distributed.

The series invites conceptual and practical contributions focused on different issue domains, policy fields, *causes célèbres*, functional processes, etc. to the extent that they contribute to sharpening the new apparatus associated with collaborative decentred metagovernance.

In the last few decades, a need has been felt for a more sophisticated understanding of the governing of the private, public and social sectors, for less compartmentalization among sectors that have much in common, and for new conceptual tools to suggest new relevant questions and new ways to carry on the business of governing by creatively recombining the tools of governance that have proved successful in all these sectors. These efforts have generated experiments that have been sufficiently rich and wide-ranging in the various laboratories to warrant efforts to pull together what we know at this stage.

The first volume in the series has scoped out in a provisional way the sort of general terrain we are going to explore. It is meant to loosely identify the horizons and the frontiers, as we perceived them at the time of launching this journey. Horizons and frontiers are not ways to limit the inquiries, but rather invitations to all forms of transgression.

The second volume provides a critical analysis of the immigration regime in Canada over the last decades and sketches ways in which it might be reformed.

Interested parties are invited to join the Chautauqua.

– Editorial Board

Titles published by Invenire are listed at the end of the book.

# Gilles Paquet

## Moderato cantabile

Toward principled governance
for Canada's immigration regime

**Collaborative Decentred Metagovernance Series**

INVENIRE BOOKS

Ottawa, Canada

2012

**University of Ottawa Press**
Les **Presses** de l'Université d'Ottawa

The University of Ottawa Press (UOP) is proud to be the oldest of the francophone university presses in Canada and the oldest bilingual university publisher in North America. Since 1936, UOP has been enriching intellectual and cultural discourse by producing peer-reviewed and award-winning books in the humanities and social sciences, in French and in English.

www.Press.uOttawa.ca

Library and Archives Canada Cataloguing in Publication

Title: Moderato cantabile : toward principled governance for Canada's immigration regime / Gilles Paquet.
Names: Paquet, Gilles, author.
Series: Collaborative decentred metagovernance series.
Description: Series statement: Collaborative decentred metagovernance series | Reprint. Originally published: Ottawa, Canada : Invenire, 2012. | Includes bibliographical references.
Identifiers: Canadiana (print) 2022038973X | Canadiana (ebook) 20220389772 | ISBN 9780776638461 (softcover) | ISBN 9780776638485 (EPUB) | ISBN 9780776638478 (PDF)
Subjects: LCSH: Canada—Emigration and immigration. | LCSH: Canada—Emigration and immigration— Government policy.
Classification: LCC JV7233 .P36 2022 | DDC 325.71—dc23

Legal Deposit: Library and Archives Canada, Third Quarter 2022
© University of Ottawa Press 2022, all rights reserved.

This book was initially published by Invenire Books in 2012 in the Collaborative Decentered Metagovernance Series. The cover design, layout and design were produced by Sandy Lynch. The University of Ottawa Press reissued this book thanks to the support of Ontario Creates.

## Invenire

Invenire Books, an Ottawa-based idea factory that operated from 2010 to 2019, specialized in collaborative governance and stewardship. Invenire and its authors provide creative practical and stimulating responses to the challenges and opportunities faced by today's organizations. The list is now carried by the University of Ottawa Press.

Profession: Public Servant
The Entrepreneurial Effect: Practical Ideas from Your Own Virtual Board of Advisors
La flotte blanche : histoire de la compagnie de navigation du Richelieu et d'Ontario
Tableau d'avancement II : essais exploratoires sur la gouvernance d'un certain Canada français
The Entrepreneurial Effect: Waterloo
The Unimagined Canadian Capital: Challenges for the Federal Capital Region
The State in Transition: Challenges for Canadian Federalism
Cities as Crucibles: Reflections on Canada's Urban Future
Gouvernance communautaire : innovations dans le Canada français hors Québec
Through the Detox Prism: Exploring Organizational Failures and Design Responses
Cities and Languages: Governance and Policy – An International Symposium
Villes et langues : gouvernance et politiques – symposium international
Moderato Cantabile: Toward Principled Governance for Canada's Immigration Policy
Stewardship: Collaborative Decentred Metagovernance and Inquiring Systems
Challenges in Public Health Governance: The Canadian Experience
Innovation in Canada: Why We Need More and What We Must Do to Get It
Challenges of Minority Governments in Canada
Gouvernance corporative : une entrée en matières

Tackling Wicked Policy Problems: Equality, Diversity and Sustainability
50 ans de bilinguisme officiel : défis, analyses et témoignages
Unusual Suspects: Essays on Social Learning
Probing the Bureaucratic Mind: About Canadian Federal Executives
Tableau d'avancement III : pour une diaspora canadienne-française antifragile
Autour de Chantal Mouffe : le politique en conflit
Town and Crown: An Illustrated History of Canada's Capital
The Tainted-Blood Tragedy in Canada: A Cascade of Governance Failures
Intelligent Governance: A Prototype for Social Coordination
Driving the Fake Out of Public Administration: Detoxing HR in the Canadian Federal Public Sector
Tableau d'avancement IV : un Canada français à ré-inventer
A Future for Economics: More Encompassing, More Institutional, More Practical
Pasquinade en F : essais à rebrousse-poil
Building Bridges: Case Studies in Collaborative Governance in Canada
Scheming Virtuously: The Road to Collaborative Governance
A Lantern on the Bow: A History of the Science Council of Canada and its Contributions to the Science and Innovation Policy Debate
Fifty Years of Official Bilingualism: Challenges, Analyses and Testimonies
Irregular Governance: A Plea for Bold Organizational Experimentation
Pasquinade in E: Slaughtering Some Sacred Cows

The University of Ottawa Press gratefully acknowledges the support extended to its publishing list by the Government of Canada, the Canada Council for the Arts, the Ontario Arts Council, the Social Sciences and Humanities Research Council and the Canadian Federation for the Humanities and Social Sciences through the Awards to Scholarly Publications Program, and by the University of Ottawa.

ONTARIO ARTS COUNCIL
CONSEIL DES ARTS DE L'ONTARIO
an Ontario government agency
un organisme du gouvernement de l'Ontario

Canada Council    Conseil des arts
for the Arts       du Canada

Canadä

uOttawa

"…for the hundredth time, it means 'moderately and melodiously'."

– *Marguerite Duras*

# Table of Contents

**Introduction** . . . . . . . . . . . . . . . . . . . . . . . . . . . . . . . . . . . . . . . . . . 1

**Chapter 1** . . . . . . . . . . . . . . . . . . . . . . . . . . . . . . . . . . . . . . . . . 11
Dumbfounding Aspects of Canadian Immigration Policy
Introduction . . . . . . . . . . . . . . . . . . . . . . . . . . . . . . . . . . . . . . . 11
Some stylized facts . . . . . . . . . . . . . . . . . . . . . . . . . . . . . . . . . 16
The baffling 'Canadian consensus' reversal after
   the mid-1990s . . . . . . . . . . . . . . . . . . . . . . . . . . . . . . . . . . . 20
A frontal attack on this wicked problem
   may be counterproductive . . . . . . . . . . . . . . . . . . . . . . . . 27
Scheming virtuously on three fronts: a brief sketch . . . . . . 28
Conclusion . . . . . . . . . . . . . . . . . . . . . . . . . . . . . . . . . . . . . . . 31

**Chapter 2** . . . . . . . . . . . . . . . . . . . . . . . . . . . . . . . . . . . . . . . . 33
Immigration and the Solidarity-Diversity-Security Nexus
Introduction . . . . . . . . . . . . . . . . . . . . . . . . . . . . . . . . . . . . . . 33
The SDS nexus . . . . . . . . . . . . . . . . . . . . . . . . . . . . . . . . . . . . 34
Citizenship and the SDS nexus . . . . . . . . . . . . . . . . . . . . . . 45
Conclusion . . . . . . . . . . . . . . . . . . . . . . . . . . . . . . . . . . . . . . . 53

**Chapter 3** . . . . . . . . . . . . . . . . . . . . . . . . . . . . . . . . . . . . . . . . 55
Toward Fair Play and Hospitality as a New Frame of Reference
Introduction . . . . . . . . . . . . . . . . . . . . . . . . . . . . . . . . . . . . . . 55
Moral revolution → social transformation . . . . . . . . . . . . . . 59
Frame of reference I . . . . . . . . . . . . . . . . . . . . . . . . . . . . . . . . 60
Common public culture under threat . . . . . . . . . . . . . . . . . . 66
Frame of reference II in the making . . . . . . . . . . . . . . . . . . . 68
Conclusion . . . . . . . . . . . . . . . . . . . . . . . . . . . . . . . . . . . . . . . 78

**Chapter 4** . . . . . . . . . . . . . . . . . . . . . . . . . . . . . . . . . . . . . . . . . 79
**Toward Principled Governance of the Immigration Regime**
   Introduction . . . . . . . . . . . . . . . . . . . . . . . . . . . . . . . . . . . . . . . 79
   Basic philosophy . . . . . . . . . . . . . . . . . . . . . . . . . . . . . . . . . . 80
   A circumspect appraisal of the state of play
      by officialdom . . . . . . . . . . . . . . . . . . . . . . . . . . . . . . . . . . 85
   Toward a new Canadian immigration regime . . . . . . . . . . 88
   The moral contracts with newcomers. . . . . . . . . . . . . . . . . 94
   Terms of integration and default settings . . . . . . . . . . . . . 103
   Conclusion . . . . . . . . . . . . . . . . . . . . . . . . . . . . . . . . . . . . . . 106

**Conclusion** . . . . . . . . . . . . . . . . . . . . . . . . . . . . . . . . . . . . . . . . . 109

**References** . . . . . . . . . . . . . . . . . . . . . . . . . . . . . . . . . . . . . . . . . 115

# | Introduction

*"… maximum is not optimum…"*
*– Garrett Hardin*

Over the last quarter of a century, Canada has become engaged in an immigration policy experiment of momentous importance, as is clear from Figure 1. The more recent data (over 280,000 immigrants in 2010 and a targeted level for 2011 of approximately 250,000) show that there has been a sustained quantum leap in immigration, vis-à-vis the pre-1990 level, which is now firmly established.

FIGURE 1:
## Number of immigrants into Canada

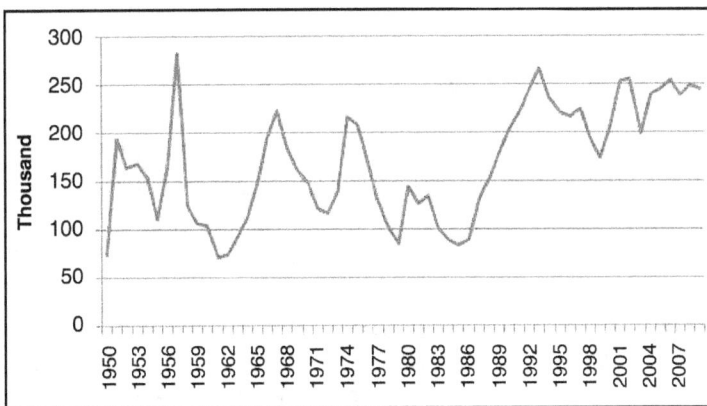

*Source: Statistics Canada, Table 075-001-Historical Statistics, 2009.*

These immigrants (of which close to one quarter are in the family reunification class) are only a portion of the new entrants into Canada each year. To these must be added, in recent years, an annual flow of a quarter of a million temporary workers, of well over 100,000 foreign students, and over 20,000 refugee claimants.

For all sorts of reasons – some understandable (if debatable), others more puzzling – Canada has opened the floodgates of immigration to such a degree that it annually allows into the country proportionally at least twice as many newcomers as most other industrialized countries. At this pace, close to one third of the population of Canada will be foreign born, and a clear majority of the population of the main Canadian cities will be foreign born by 2030.

The initiative is sufficiently important for one to presume that it has been the result of a reasoned discussion at its inception, or to expect that at least now it is on the agenda of most Canadian political parties or think-tanks, as the consequences (financial, economic, social and cultural) of this initiative are becoming a bit clearer. Surprisingly, the issue was not seriously discussed then, nor is it now, because it has been and, remains, a taboo topic.

This lack of critical thinking is mainly due to a parallel initiative originating in Canada in the 1970s – multiculturalism – a policy that went into high gear in the early 1980s, when the Charter of Rights and Freedoms stipulated that the Charter "shall be interpreted in a manner consistent with the preservation and enhancement of the multicultural heritage of Canadians."[1] In entrenching the multiculturalism commitment in the Charter, the Canadian government *de facto* excluded this policy from being a discussable subject in Ottawa.

The full impact of multiculturalism-cum-Charter was felt in the 1980s and early 1990s, as a result of an impressive propaganda machine – some state-funded, some rooted in flawed 'progressive' political philosophies – that transformed the multiculturalism policy and its circumstances into part of

---

[1] Charter of Rights and Freedoms, Article 27, 1982.

the 'Canada brand.' At the time, any critical comment became not only unwelcome, but also effectively denounced.

This prepared the ground for two decades of massive and indiscriminate immigration flows that were much larger than Canada could reasonably absorb. The financial and economic costs of this policy (that allowed more and more immigrants, refugees and temporary workers into the country without regard to the country's socio-economic situation or its carrying capacity) have been significant, not only for Canadian-born, but also for the newcomers.[2]

Data marshalled by Patrick Grady and his colleagues have shown that the more recent cohorts of newcomers have suffered mightily; each successive cohort of immigrants (even those with a higher level of education and competence) over the last 20 years has had more and more difficulty integrating successfully into Canada's socio-economy, and has found its level of welfare falling more and more vis-à-vis the level of welfare of the Canadian-born.[3] As Grady mentions, "in a welfare state like Canada, if immigrants don't do at least as well economically as other Canadians, they will pay less tax and receive greater government benefits." The net annual fiscal cost for Canada has been estimated as falling in the range of $16 to $23 billion, depending on the number of immigrants assumed to remain in the country.[4] Less easily calculated are the social, cultural and security costs of this massive and indiscriminate immigration: they have probably been even greater as ethnic enclaves grew around the country, and some serious strains on the common public culture have been recorded.

There is not a single source for the problems of economic and social integration of the recent newcomers. For instance,

[2] A very comprehensive and thoughtful brief has been submitted by Patrick Grady on behalf of the Centre for Immigration Policy Reform. Patrick Grady. September 2011. *Immigration is Too High and Not Based on Canada's Economic Interests: A Submission to the Stakeholder and Public Consultation on Immigration Levels and Mix.* www.immigrationreform.ca.

[3] Patrick Grady, 2011, p. 3.

[4] Herbert Grubel and Patrick Grady. 2011. "Immigration and the Welfare State 2011," *Studies in Immigration and Refugee Policy.* Vancouver: Fraser Institute.

the ethnic and country-of-origin composition of the flows has changed over that period; this most certainly has made integration more difficult. But this is obviously a matter that should have been taken into account in assessing the absorptive capacity of the country. Moreover, in the last 20 years, Canada has experienced many spells of recession that have been merrily ignored by policy makers and during which immigration flows have been maintained at extraordinary levels. Given all this, the pace of immigration has accelerated unduly.

There have been crass motivations to ignore the pre-cautionary principle and to support the massive and indiscriminate immigration policy. It has been seen as yielding much electoral capital for political parties in a country where some 20 percent of the population is foreign born, and a substantial portion of this group has only arrived in Canada post World War II and still has deep connections with their country of origin. Such excessive immigration has also put downward pressure on wages and is a significant source of revenue for immigration lawyers.

But there has also been an ideological drive behind the push for massive and indiscriminate immigration flows. It has been driven by a canonical discourse based on a number of false assumptions about immigration being: (1) the source of significant economic growth and welfare; (2) a cure for the aging structure of the population (and essential to ensure that pensioners will continue to receive their cheques); and (3) the obvious way to pursue diversity as an absolute social good. These arguments have been effectively disposed of by economists, demographers and other social scientists, but with little impact on conventional wisdom.[5]

Not everyone has been blind and deaf in the face of such dysfunctions and disinformation. These issues have been the source of a *malaise* that has been expressed in a somewhat muted voice because (especially since the 1990s) any public

[5] Patrick Grady, 2011; Gilles Paquet. 2008. *Deep Cultural Diversity – A Governance Challenge.* Ottawa. University of Ottawa Press; Benoît Dubreuil and Guillaume Marois. 2011. *Le remède imaginaire.* Montreal: Boréal.

statement about it has been regarded as politically incorrect. More recently, however, louder grumblings have been heard. But the sentiment of many opinion makers (business executives, journalists, 'progressive' academics and the like) is not aligned to the views of the public on such matters: the former would appear to remain largely supportive of massive and accelerated immigration, while the latter hold the view that the pace of immigration should be contained. Even an otherwise thoughtful journalist like John Ibbitson has argued for increasing the annual immigration flows to over 400,000;[6] and former federal Liberal minister, Robert Kaplan, has also defended its desirability in order to grow Canada to a population of 100 million by 2100.

There is still an immense amount of cognitive dissonance cluttering the Canadian mind on these issues. The arguments that the optimal immigration flow may not be the maximum immigration flow; that Canada should admit newcomers only on the basis of its well understood social, economic and cultural absorptive capacity and of a much tighter selection process; and, that there are limits to diversity, have still not gotten through to the Canadian intelligentsia.

The fact that Canada's extraordinary immigration gamble has received so little critical scrutiny by the intelligentsia has allowed a nexus of economic and ideological pro-immigration interests (businesses in search of cheap labour, immigration lawyers and the like, diversity crusaders, etc.) to pressure Canadian governments to make ever bolder and more irresponsible moves on this front. Consequently, there is some urgency to expose the foundational myths on which such an immigration regime has been erected, and to propose a palatable alternative to the current approach.

This must be done before the Canadian population (generally an immigrant-friendly population that, for generations, has welcomed newcomers in very large but workable numbers

[6] John Ibbitson. 2005. *The Polite Revolution – Perfecting the Canadian Dream.* Toronto: McClelland & Stewart, p. 111. Ibbitson sees massive and indiscriminate immigration on this aggrandized scale as a way to stop what he calls, in a somewhat melodramatic way, "demographic suicide" (*Globe & Mail*, August 19, 2011, A13).

given the circumstances) becomes disenchanted through the refusal to discuss critically the toxic impact of the current massive and indiscriminate immigration.

Chapter 1 presents a broad-brushed statement of some dumbfounding aspects of Canada's immigration policy: a probing of the dramatic and puzzling Canadian reversal of opinion on the matter of immigration after the mid-80s (toward support for massive immigration); a look at recent signs of an obverse reversal in the making; a sketch of a possibly fruitful and more enlightened approach to a critical discussion of the costs and benefits of the recent immigration policy; and, of the foundations of a principled immigration regime.

Chapter 2 probes the solidarity-diversity-security trade-offs in the design of an immigration regime. This is intended to illustrate some of the various dimensions that have to be traded off in arriving at a reasonable immigration regime. It exposes the sophistry used to defend the present massive and indiscriminate immigration policy and the costs of inaction by not countering this irresponsible stand.

Chapter 3 recognizes that the broad suggestions for reform in chapters 1 and 2 have little chance to materialize unless the intellectual foundations of the existing regime are challenged. The current cosmology must be questioned and an alternative philosophy proposed that can carry the accord of the Canadian population. This entails both a demolition and reconstruction job: first, some questioning of the fragile basis of the ideology of multiculturalism and of the trolley of rights and entitlements it has come to underpin in bolstering the immigration regime in good currency; and second, some suggestions as to what might constitute a more defendable alternative set of principles on which to erect a more socially acceptable and more sound immigration regime. This leads to an examination and defence of the principles of fair play and hospitality as a foundation from which one can derive some guideposts for a principled immigration regime.

Chapter 4 develops those guideposts. The intent is less to provide a ready-made detailed blueprint of an immigration policy that would be perfectly adjusted to the present season, than to design an **inquiring system** based on a broad set of standards that can help to critically assess many of the features of the current regime, and serve as a guide in redefining our immigration policy over time. The immigration regime needs to adjust to changing internal and external circumstances, while ensuring that it unfolds in a manner that respects the integrity of the host society and the foundational principles and norms that society wishes to preserve.

In the conclusion, it is argued that the Canadian cosmology in good currency over the last few decades may not collapse under its own inadequacies until it is too late, unless an alternative is sharply put forward. What is required is the emergence of an **intermediate-cosmopolitanism social movement** and some cultural change that will transform our code of honour – our notion of what it is that we regard as an honourable way to act.

This short book is a sequel to my *Deep Cultural Diversity – A Governance Challenge* published in 2008.[7] In the earlier volume, I was interested mainly in the phenomenon of diversity, and the discussion was only peripherally engaged with the immigration regime. I tried to make the point that diversity was not an absolute good and that policies based on a blind pursuit of maximum diversity – without due attention being given to an appreciation of its economic, socio-political and cultural impacts – were likely to founder in Canada and elsewhere. I then suggested ways in which one might optimize and regulate diversity. In so doing, I commented in passing on the general lack of wisdom regarding massive and indiscriminate immigration, but that was not the main focus of this earlier work.

In the present volume, the immigration regime is the core issue of interest, and Canada's gamble over the past 25 years is the experiment of concern. If some lessons for other countries may be derived from our discussion, all the better, but Canada has pursued a rather unique path in the immigration file and that calls for special attention. Only in Canada has the pursuit of diversity become an ideological crusade and a sort of fetish

[7] Gilles Paquet, 2008.

vigorously marketed by the government of Canada as its brand over the last few decades.

The multiculturalism policy had originally been adopted in the 1970s for crass electoral reasons and as a way to diffuse the hold of the two-founding-nation paradigm that irked Pierre Trudeau so much. This took on a new twist as the proportion of the population born abroad grew to over 20 percent, and to twice as much in some large cities. Immigrant groups were encouraged by lax rules (allowing them to bring to Canada members of their very extended family) to believe that such rules should be used and could be abused.[8] But it would not have been possible to 'sell' the rest of the Canadian citizenry on massive and indiscriminate immigration – at least enough to explain the phenomenal growth of the support for massive and indiscriminate immigration between 1986 and 2005 – without the diversity/multiculturalism propaganda push.

The 'Canada brand' supplied the intellectual basis for the new policy and provided a protective belt against any frontal attack on the new immigration regime by those who had become conscious of its various costs. The present volume questions the feeble intellectual foundations of such a policy, but aims also, and most importantly, to engineer a transformation of this intellectual basis in order to allow a more honest discussion of a reasonable immigration regime to become possible and legitimate.

In the period during which this project has been carried out, I have received much help in terms of data, information and intelligence about the Canadian immigration regime from some colleagues at the Canadian Centre for Immigration Policy Reform, and also some cautious moral support – cautious because, even though they most certainly share my concerns, many of them do not necessarily support my suggestions. My étapiste, moderate and melodious approach to the problems, has not swayed all of them and some feel that more draconian

---

[8] This has led to championships: a Somali-born Canadian who brought 100 members of his family to Canada in the last decade (*CBC News*. July 21, 2011).

action is required. So, fellow members of the Centre should not be tarred with any scorn or guilt by association.

I have also received timid comments from academic colleagues, who neither share my concerns nor support my line of argument. On the one hand, their stern politeness in listening to my arguments is a testimony to their patience, and for that I am grateful. On the other hand, their failure to persuade me that their Panglossian counter-arguments held water (especially that there has not been a change of kind in the Canadian immigration regime in the last decades and that, in any case, all problems are bound to disappear with the second generation) has been a source of reassurance that I may have a point, and for that I am grateful, too.

# CHAPTER 1

# | Dumbfounding Aspects of Canadian Immigration Policy

*"...unsettling or rash lack of concern..."*
*(the definition of criminal negligence*
*in the Canadian Criminal Code)*

## Introduction

There are many reasons why immigration flows may be said to be welfare-enhancing for a community (skilled immigrants add value) and many reasons why national governments may wish to actively promote immigration. But there are no reasons to believe that maximum indiscriminate immigration is an automatic optimum. Massive international migration flows may be disruptive and welfare-reducing for the host country. This is the case even when political, social, cultural, humanitarian, and all other sorts of benefits and costs (over and beyond the financial dimensions) are taken into account. There is no reason to believe that massive, indiscriminate migration flows can be regarded as automatically desirable as a national policy. It all depends on the balance of costs and benefits.

Yet over the last 25 years, Canada has apparently adopted such an immigration policy based on a "faith in the long term benefits of high levels of immigration," although no evidence or meaningful argument has ever been put forward to justify this faith,[9] and there are reasons to believe that it serves neither the newcomers nor Canadian society well.

The only political rationale to explain this new philosophy of immigration is that it appears to have been a seductive tactic to get the vote of the roughly 20 percent of the Canadian population that is foreign-born – a segment of the population that is purported to benefit from family reunification and the 'chain immigration' this process underpins.

This new era followed decades when the Canadian immigration policy had been defined in keeping with what was called **the absorptive capacity of the Canadian socio-economy**. Such a stance seems to have served both Canada and the newcomers well, since it can be demonstrated that the Canadian experience of integration proved quite successful: newcomers integrated into the Canadian socio-economy well and relatively quickly, and contributed significantly and positively to their new homeland.

Surprisingly, this act of faith in the long-term benefits of much higher levels of immigration has not been challenged as one might have expected, even though economists have argued for more than 20 years that economic benefits are likely to be very small.[10] This unfounded assertion continues to be presented as self-evident by many stakeholders and so-called 'progressives.' It has even come to be consecrated by some political scientists like Keith Banting as corresponding to **a Canadian consensus.**[11]

According to Jeffrey Reitz, this **Canadian consensus in support of massive indiscriminate immigration** is supposedly based on two pillars:[12] first, "belief in immigration as economic

[9] Alan Green and David Green. 2004. "The Goals of Canada's Immigration Policy: A Historical Perspective," *Canadian Journal of Urban Research*, 13(1): 102-139.

[10] Economic Council of Canada. 1991. *New Faces in the Crowd*. Ottawa: Supply & Services.

[11] Quoted by journalist Peter O'Neil. September 25, 2010. "Is Canada up to the Immigration Challenge?" *Ottawa Citizen*, A6.

[12] Jeffrey G. Reitz. May 20, 2011. "Immigration: The United States v Canada," *The Economist*; Jeffrey G. Reitz. 2011. *Pro-Immigration Canada – Social and Economic Roots of Popular Views*. Montreal: Institute for Research on Public Policy.

benefit" (because they have been told repeatedly that, through the operation of the point system selection process, the newcomers are highly skilled and therefore must be net contributors to Canadian wealth enhancement); and second, "pride in Canadian multiculturalism" because, supposedly, Canadians have been persuaded by the 'multiculturalism commitment' to view **diversity, *per se*, as a very important primary good** and have developed a pride in this becoming a Canada brand. So even if the positive economic benefits could be put in doubt, such accelerated immigration inflows could still be presumed to have by definition an overall positive impact since they contribute to the diversity objective. As a matter of consequence, any suggestion that such an immigration regime could have a negative impact on the security and health of Canadians, on solidarity and the Canadian social fabric, or on the commitment to the welfare state or other fundamental institutions in the host society, has been merrily discounted.

This Panglossian view, based on ill-founded assumptions but robust state propaganda, has been contested in some circles.[13] But much of the criticism has been denounced in progressive circles and the media as racist, nativist and even fascist and, in official circles, as politically incorrect.

I will argue that Canadians have been: (1) disinformed systematically by officials and the media about the real impact on the economy of massive immigration, and about its use to counter the effects of the aging of the Canadian population, and (2) hoodwinked by state-sponsored multiculturalism into accepting diversity as an unbounded blessing when, in fact, the optimum amount of diversity is not necessarily maximum diversity, because maximum diversity could have negative impacts on many aspects of the host society, including the common public culture.

---

[13] Gilles Paquet. 2008. *Deep Cultural Diversity – A Governance Challenge*. Ottawa: University of Ottawa Press; Gilles Paquet. 2010. "Immigration and the Solidarity-Diversity-Security Nexus," *www.optimumonline.ca*, 40(4): 73-93. See also the website of the Centre for Immigration Policy Reform (www. immigrationreform.ca).

These unfounded assumptions have been presented as self-evident by a diffuse coalition of immigration activists and naïve academics (with the complicity of politicians) to fuel a vicious cycle: the high percentage of foreign-born in the population triggering more pressure for increased immigration (whatever the consequences) as politicians try to capture the electoral support of these new Canadians.

The myths of immigration generating economic benefits and demographic correction to Canada's age structure, and of desirable diversity as a 'Canada brand,' have been drummed into Canadians' psyche to such an extent that it has become conventional wisdom. There is no reason to believe that this dynamic will not continue unbounded. All the more so when it is anticipated that by 2031 the foreign-born component should reach between one-quarter and one-third of the total Canadian population, according to official Canadian government forecasts.

The lack of critical debate about immigration is significant, not only because of greater economic costs than benefits (although the imbalance on this front is enormous), but also because massive and indiscriminate immigration is being allowed to somewhat irresponsibly redefine the very Canadian common public culture – its references, norms, and social codes. The deity of diversity and state-promoted multiculturalism as ideological programming about cultural relativism, equality of cultures, and the commitment to the "preservation and enhancement of the multicultural heritage of Canadians" have transformed Canada's self-image, its identity, and even the way in which public institutions would appear to react to critical events. We are no longer debating matters of degree here, but matters of kind.[14]

---

[14] These matters are always difficult to gauge but careful observers of the Canadian scene have noted that transformation (Andrew Cohen. 2007. *The Unfinished Canadian*. Toronto: McClelland & Steward, chapter 5). For a more general discussion of such transformations, see George A. Akerlof and Rachel E. Kranton. 2010. *Identity Economics*. Princeton: Princeton University Press. Recent events around the Shafia affair (Afghan-Canadian parents convicted of honour killing in the death of their three daughters) have also led commentators to speculate on the fact that public officials would appear

In summary, my argument suggests that:

- there can be no denial that the current Canadian immigration and refugee regime supports massive and indiscriminate immigration;[15]

- there is something puzzling about the so-called 'pan-Canadian consensus' that materialized between the mid-1990s and the mid-2000s (from a position where two-thirds of Canadians polled consistently found immigration levels to be too high, to a position where two-thirds of Canadians polled disagreed with this statement). This reversal of position is most certainly not evidence-based, and it happened at times of increasing immigration flows and increasing difficulties of integration for newcomers. There are reasons to believe that it has been nurtured by naïve multiculturalists, immigration activists, and the state's deepening multiculturalist propaganda. As Andrew Cohen suggests, "if enough people tell you this, you come to believe it;"[16]

- while the federal Liberal Party played a key role in early targeting the vote of the foreign-born by favouring mass immigration, by the end of the first decade of the 21st century, all political parties had been forced to follow suit for these same electoral reasons. An examination of the electoral literature of all parties in the May 2011 federal election is illuminating;

---

to have been slow and numb in reacting to the call for help of the Shafia sisters in Montreal, when the same sort of family violence in a '*Québecois de souche*' family would have most certainly triggered more intrusive and robust action. It is legitimate to ask whether cultural relativism has already permeated the *manière de voir* of officialdom and whether it has led to a degree of tolerance in the name of 'cultural difference' that could be responsible for criminal tolerance (Christie Blatchford. November 25, 2011. "Trial shows system numb to abuse," *Ottawa Citizen*; Richard Martineau. November 26, 2011. "Une tragédie évitable?" *Le Journal de Montréal*).

[15] Some have argued that the existence of a point system means that the immigration regime is not indiscriminate. However the evidence collected on the laxity with which the system is used and administered is sufficient for one to have great doubt about its effectiveness.

[16] Andrew Cohen, 2007, p. 158.

- many serious cost-benefit analyses of the new policy reveal that the costs are greater than the benefits and that, therefore it is welfare-reducing for Canadian society; in addition there are other deleterious effects in terms of health, security, solidarity, etc.;
- there has been much sophistry and deception in defending the new policy by sheer disinformation, yet it is surreptitiously redefining the Canadian identity and, in the name of political correctness, there is a systematic suppression of any critical discussion about the new norms; and
- much administrative pathology has developed as a result of this new policy being recklessly carried out – for example, an ever laxer selection process, fraud, etc., ascribable to administrative overload.

As a result, there are good reasons to believe that this new policy serves neither Canadian society nor the newcomers well, and that it must be reformed. Consequently, a three-pronged counter-attack would seem to be warranted:

1. the demolition of some toxic myths in good currency;
2. an exposé of the most grievous administrative pathologies (in particular, those around the selection process, etc.); and
3. an effort be made to free the forum from the taboo that has been imposed on any discussion about immigration and diversity in Canada, so as to break the mould of political correctness and the hold that the newly 'manufactured consensus' has on the public mind.

## Some stylized facts

The following sample of puzzling (and potentially bothersome) features of the Canadian immigration and refugee regimes is common knowledge. These facts have been documented (and at times denounced) over the years in various studies:[17]

[17] Martin Collacott. 2003. *Canada's Immigration Policy: The Need for Major Reform.* Vancouver: The Fraser Institute; Herbert Grubel (ed.). 2009. *The Effects of Mass Immigration on Canadian Living Standards and Society.* Vancouver: The Fraser Institute; Robin Banerjee and William B.P. Robson. 2009. *Faster, Younger,*

- for the past 20 years we have been accepting numbers close to one percent of our population as official immigrants each year, i.e., circa 280,000 last year (without counting temporary workers, foreign students and refugees);
- in the last 25 years, the number of immigrants has increased systematically without any regard to the employment and economic conditions in Canada;
- the United States admits half as many official immigrants on a per capita basis as Canada, and their best experts have recommend that their immigration flow should be cut in half,[18] because it is not helping economic growth;
- 80 percent of our official immigrants are not in the skilled-worker category;
- only 17 percent of the 'principal' applicants in the selected worker category are chosen for their potential to enter the workforce;
- only one-fifth of the selected immigrants are met face-to-face and interviewed by a visa officer before being admitted to the country;
- the economic situation of the more recent cohorts of immigrants vis-à-vis the Canadian-born has dramatically deteriorated over the past 20 years, thereby revealing growing difficulties of integration;
- the rate of refugee acceptance in Canada is three times the average of other countries, including a large number who would not even be considered as genuine refugees by other countries (e.g., those coming from the United States, the United Kingdom, Germany, Sweden, etc. –

*Richer? – The Fond Hope and Sobering Reality of Immigration's Impact on Canada's Demographic and Economic Future.* Toronto: C.D. Howe Institute; Centre for Immigration Policy Reform, www.immigrationreform.ca. Already in the 1990s, senior officials in Ottawa were alerting the federal minster to the looming problems. Donald A. George and Margret Kopala. 2011. "Jack Manion and his concerns about immigration policy," *www.optimumonline.ca*, 41(1): 48-49.

[18] George Borjas. 1999. *Heaven's Gate – Immigration Policy and the American Economy.* Princeton: Princeton University Press.

countries considered to have democratic regimes and sound rule of law).

Moreover, the laxity of the admissibility criteria related to health, criminality, security, etc. (that have plagued the immigration and refugee regimes since the 1990s) has been denounced vehemently by the Office of the Auditor General.[19] This laxity has made it more and more painful for newcomers to integrate effectively into the labour market, and it has led to growing frustrations. Consequently, even some immigrant groups have come to favour a reduction in the immigration level and, by a proportion of over 70 percent in some Canadian polls, are supporting the recommendation that the selection process be tightened by requiring, for instance, that newcomers be competent in English or French when they arrive.[20]

Finally, there is much cognitive dissonance in this world about immigration and diversity. Information that has become available over the last 20 years has been explicitly ignored and occluded because it fits badly with the new paradigm that underpins the indoctrination program. This has been the case for research that showed that what Canadians would gain from immigration in terms of economic benefits is very small,[21] and for the work of demographers that have argued that immigration cannot be expected to compensate for an aging population in Canada either in the short term or the long term.[22] Yet statements to the contrary continue to be constantly

[19] Martin Collacott, 2003, p. 26-33.

[20] Martin Collacott. March 10, 2010. "Immigrants Want Less Immigration." *National Post*.

[21] Economic Council of Canada, 1991.

[22] It has been shown that to maintain the current age structure of the population (i.e., to counter the aging of Canadian population by immigration), the annual immigration flows would have to be 10 times the largest annual immigration flows that Canada has ever had throughout its history. Such a scenario would entail a five-fold increase of the Canadian population over the next 50 years (to some 150 million). By comparison, Canada's population (despite the baby boom and a very large immigration) has only doubled over the last 50 years. Such a disruptive scenario is totally unthinkable. See Banerjee and Robson, 2009; Benoît Dubreuil and Guillaume Marois. 2011. *Le remède imaginaire*. Montreal: Boréal, p. 53ss.

repeated by politicians, officials, 'progressive academics' and the media. This is systematic disinformation.

Another important quantity of carefully unacknowledged information has to do with the current immigration regime resulting in an excess supply of unskilled labour, thus making integration in the Canadian labour market much more difficult, and at much lowered levels of compensation. Indeed, Statistics Canada has shown that the recent cohorts have found their integration more painful, and their earnings in relation to native Canadians significantly lower and continuing to deteriorate even further.[23] And this is true not only at the lower end of the scale. Green and Green have also shown that there has been a pressure downward on wages paid even to well-educated workers, with the immigrants themselves "struggling – with declining success – to find jobs commensurate with their knowledge and experience...."[24]

As Michael Valpy put it, this poses a question about the morality of admitting that many immigrants.[25]

Finally, there are also pernicious costs associated with the current immigration regime discouraging efforts to train and put to work Canadians who are unemployed or underemployed (e.g., Aboriginals), and there is the negative impact of the immigration regime on the development of more effective methods of production in Canada by making cheap labour available.[26]

[23] Garnett Picot et al. 2007. *Chronic Low-Income and Low-Income Dynamics among Recent Immigrants.* Statistics Canada, Catalogue No. 11f0019MIE2007198.

[24] Alan Green and David Green, 2004, p. 134.

[25] Quoted in James Bissett. 2009. "The Current State of Canadian Immigration Policy" in Herbert Grubel (ed.). *The Effects of Mass Immigration on Canadians Living Standards and Society.* Vancouver: The Fraser Institute, p. 11. See also Statistics Canada. 2007. *Impact of Immigration on Labour Markets in Canada, Mexico and the United States,* http://dsp-psd.pwgsc.gc.ca/collection_2007/statcan/89-001-XIE2007001.pdf.

[26] Daniel Stoffman. 2008. "Truths and Myths about Immigration" in Alexander Moens and Martin Collacott (eds.). *Immigration Policy and Terrorist Threat in Canada and the United States.* Vancouver: The Fraser Institute, p. 3-28.

## The baffling Canadian consensus reversal after the mid-1990s

Despite these facts, it is surprising to see a dramatic reversal of perspectives in the opinion polls with reference to immigration after the mid-1990s in Canada, i.e., at the very time when things were seriously deteriorating.

When Canadians were asked whether they agreed with the vague statement, "The economic impact of immigration is positive," some 40 percent responded NO in 1993. But to the same question in 2005, only 15 percent responded NO. Indeed, over 80 percent of Canadians polled agreed with this statement in 2005, despite the quasi-unanimous opposite view of experts. To the statement "The immigration level is too high," two-thirds of Canadians responded YES from 1977 to 1993-94 but, over the following decade, this proportion dropped to one-third; two-thirds of respondents disagreed with this proposition (see Figure 2, page 26). All this has been happening while, in the period from 1993 to today, two-thirds of the Canadians polled felt that too many immigrants do not adopt Canadian values. Even the idea that immigration takes away Canadian jobs (supported by over 90 percent of respondents in 1985) was rejected by close to 80 percent of respondents in the mid-2000s.[27]

The same two main factors (presumed economic advantages plus commitment to diversity and pride in multiculturalism) are said to explain this extraordinary reversal. The main point in contention is whether this reversal is mainly ascribable to a normal organic evolution of public opinion (echoing rapid changes in underlying values), or to disinformation and brainwashing.[28]

---

[27] All those results are extracted from various presentations made by Michael Adams and the Environics Institute over the last decades.

[28] Jeffrey G. Reitz would appear to presume that these 'popular views' are an exact reflection of underlying social values. See Jeffrey G. Reitz, 2011. This is an extraordinary presumption, for values do not usually change as dramatically and fundamentally in a few years. It would appear more reasonable to presume that there is no such 'virgin birth' of public opinion, and that in the case of immigration, in particular, there is some basis to believe that the 'popular views' have been significantly shaped by

First, existing research on the motivations at work and the process of formation of public opinion on matters of immigration shows them to be complex. But it would appear that (net of all other factors), it is **the so-called 'symbolic-political dimension'** (reflecting the dominant national discourse in Canada) that has the most important impact. The beliefs about the positive or negative impact of immigration on the nation, or the like, are seen as a major determinant of the choice for expansion or restriction of immigration.[29]

Those research results are of crucial importance for they underline the centrality of the efforts to manufacture a dominant national discourse by the clerisy of groups with an interest in immigration expansion. It is less the personal circumstances of particular individuals than the overall belief in a certain national rationale that appears to be echoed in opinion polls. Persuading the population (however false that may be) that high levels of immigration are a significant source of economic growth and welfare-enhancement for the country, and that this will contribute to rebalancing the age structure of the population (thereby helping to sustain the financial viability of the welfare state for an aging Canadian population), has had considerable force in determining the response to questions about the expansion or restriction of immigration levels.

As a result, over the last 20 years, and regardless of the socio-economic conditions, the level of the flow of new immigrants has been raised, and suggestions to tighten the selection criteria – even those recommended by the Immigration Legislative Review – were successfully opposed by immigration activists, immigrant service organizations and major political parties. This situation continued during the May 2011 federal election campaign, where all parties promised immigration levels

---

disinformation and propaganda. This is most certainly a view that can be shown to be supported by research in this issue domain, such as the work quoted in the next footnote.

[29] Jessica Fortin and Peter John Loewen. 2004. "Prejudice and Asymmetrical Opinion Structures: Public Opinion toward Immigration in Canada." Paper presented at the Annual Meeting of the Canadian Political Science Association at the University of Winnipeg, Winnipeg, MB, June 3.

higher than the 2010 levels – when 280,000 immigrants had been received – at a time when Canada had just lost close to half a million full-time jobs because of the recession – all because 80 percent of Canadians polled had clearly been led to believe (falsely) that high levels of immigration would generate economic growth and correct the demographic imbalance.

These false beliefs were drummed into the Canadian consciousness by officials and other opinion-moulders. Since this is a debate with a certain degree of technical complexity, Canadian citizens have not necessarily invested the requisite time to be able to appreciate the arguments and have relied on the apparent consensus of opinion-moulders. One can only speak of systematic disinformation by politicians and their consorts.

This disinformation became even more strident as of the mid 1990s because the electoral stakes had become higher: by that time, 20 percent of the Canadian population was foreign-born and, in the cases of Toronto and Vancouver, the proportion was coming close to 50 percent and 40 percent, respectively. Among the major political parties, it was a case of which one would sound more pro-immigration, and there was implicit collusion among the political parties to prevent any serious discussion of the evidence presented that seemed to suggest action to the contrary.

Second, it is not clear that this coalition of disinformers would have been anything like as successful as it has been were it not for the aggressive way in which the philosophy of multiculturalism was bolstered by the Charter of Rights of 1982. This began to bear fruit in the 1980s (the Singh case) when it was argued, invoking the Charter, that once a newcomer put his foot on Canadian soil (legally or not), he could claim entitlement to all the rights of Canadians, except the right to vote. This contention was supported by the Supreme Court of Canada and, as a matter of consequence, Canada lost control of her borders. The Mulroney government could not persuade itself to invoke the notwithstanding clause to defer the application of the decision of the Supreme Court of Canada, for Charter activism had already given a new wind to multiculturalism.

This movement came to full maturity in the 1990s and was accompanied by an extraordinary effort to propagandize and celebrate multiculturalism, and to theorize it as not only 'progressive,' and changing the very nature of the social game (and therefore of Canadian identity), but also as a model for the rest of the world.[30] It is not so much that the books of Charles Taylor and Will Kymlicka triggered the movement: they simply echoed the very active multiculturalist propaganda that had permeated *le pouvoir social* in Canada and theorized it, thereby granting legitimacy to the on-going transformation of the social norms. Indeed, this propagandizing aimed at making multiculturalism a source of national pride; unity in diversity became the mantra and a subject of some naïve sort of exultation.[31] The full implications of this leap of faith may not have been understood by the host population, but they were fully grasped by the newcomers as a powerful lever.

What Tocqueville called *le pouvoir social* connotes the mechanisms through which, on certain topics or issues, a dominant view (however ill-founded it may be) comes to prevail, and to become a dominant view, in the face of which even substantive criticism is impotent.[32] In the case of multiculturalism, the chorus of interest groups, intelligentsia and the media effectively presented it as 'progressive' and therefore desirable. Eventually, such a view becomes a sort of conventional wisdom. The Canadian *pouvoir social* has been imbibed by the philosophy of multiculturalism. This has led to a growing reluctance to challenge this iconic issue, to the point where anyone doing so faced various forms of censorship.

[30] Charles Taylor. 1992. *Multiculturalism and the Politics of Recognition*. Princeton: Princeton University Press; Will Kimlicka. 1995. *Multinational Citizenship – A Liberal Theory of Minority Rights*. New York: Oxford University Press.

[31] The centrality of such pride is granted by Jeffery G. Reitz, 2011, but is presented as a result of a process of 'immaculate conception' and not as ascribable to propaganda.

[32] Raymond Boudon. 2005. *Tocqueville aujourd'hui*. Paris: Odile Jacob, p. 167-175.

One can reasonably refer to this period as one where the Canadian identity was surreptitiously transformed, where the reference points were modified, and where a new *ethos* came to be dramatically redefined in terms of 'new truths.' Not only were new ideals and norms being brandished, but these new ideals were also articulated in a language of rights and became immunized from any criticism by their Charter base.[33]

Both as a result of a change in the composition of the population, and of a mix of disinformation and propaganda to promote the so-called Canadian way, groundless beliefs (immigration has a significant positive economic impact and can correct the age structure imbalance created by the aging of the Canadian population, and diversity for the sake of diversity is an absolute good and aggressive pursuit of it a sign of moral superiority one can be proud of) have come to dominate the national discourse. Moreover, any opposition to these beliefs is met with a certain amount of social odium. So, it is misleading to speak of a 'consensus' that would have emerged by 'virgin birth.' Deception is why Canadian citizens support that policy.

In an era of growing moral relativism, this sort of propaganda has led to *insouciance* about the very notion of a Canadian common public culture, of Canada's cultural traits deserving to be preserved, and to cultural relativism. This frame of mind is starkly illustrated by the advertising brochure circulated in the 1980s and 1990s by the Secretary of State that advised prospective immigrants that they could bring their own culture with them when they migrated to Canada because Canada had no culture of its own![34]

---

[33] For a general discussion of the ways in which people and organizations may manipulate categories, norms and ideals, see Akerlof and Kranton, 2010, p. 124ff.

[34] Indeed, the Secretary of State for Multiculturalism, Sheila Finestone, may be said to have echoed the *zeitgeist* of the day on national TV in January 1995 when she said that "there isn't any one Canadian identity. Canada has no national culture," quoted in Richard Gwyn. 1995. *Nationalism without Walls.* Toronto: McClelland & Stewart, p. 111.

To the extent that Canadians have been re-programmed, it is now regarded as politically incorrect to hold the views they held in the 1980s, and so Canadians no longer reveal them. Therefore, one may question the meaningfulness of what is labelled the **Canadian consensus** on such issues as recorded in polls. What the polls are harvesting is nothing more than the results generated by a mix of disinformation and propaganda sown over the previous few decades.

It is interesting, in closing this section, to note two flats or sharps that would appear to give signs that the process of manufacturing the new consensus may not be as successful and permanent as might have been anticipated. They suggest that cracks in this 'consensus' are beginning to emerge.

First, the only region of the country where the massive immigration policy is being openly questioned these days (and indeed where there are open discussions about reducing the official immigration flows) is Quebec. It is the segment of the country where multiculturalism is openly contested as well. These discussions are surprising given that immigration might be regarded as a way for Quebec to maintain its political and linguistic valence within Canada – a not unimportant concern of Quebec politicians.[35]

Second, the 2010 data from polling firm, Environics, shows that there has been what might be the beginning of another significant reversal in the making between 2008 and 2010: the percentage of respondents agreeing with the statement that there is too much immigration has grown from 33 percent to 40 percent, and the percentage of those disagreeing has slipped from 63 percent to 56 percent (Figure 2). It is obviously too early to conjecture that this is the beginning of a trend, but it may suggest that the disinformation and the propaganda that I claim are very much at the basis of the manufactured public opinion

---

[35] For a recent analysis of the Quebec scene that makes reference to many of the issues raised above, see Mathieu Bock-Côté. April 2010-June 2011. *Aux origines du malaise politique québécois.* http://bock-cote.net.

may be beginning to give signs of not any longer being entirely immune to the forces of evidence.[36]

### FIGURE 2: Are immigration levels too high?
### Do you agree or disagree?

**Majority disagree that there is too much immigration, but recent spike in concern**

1977-2010

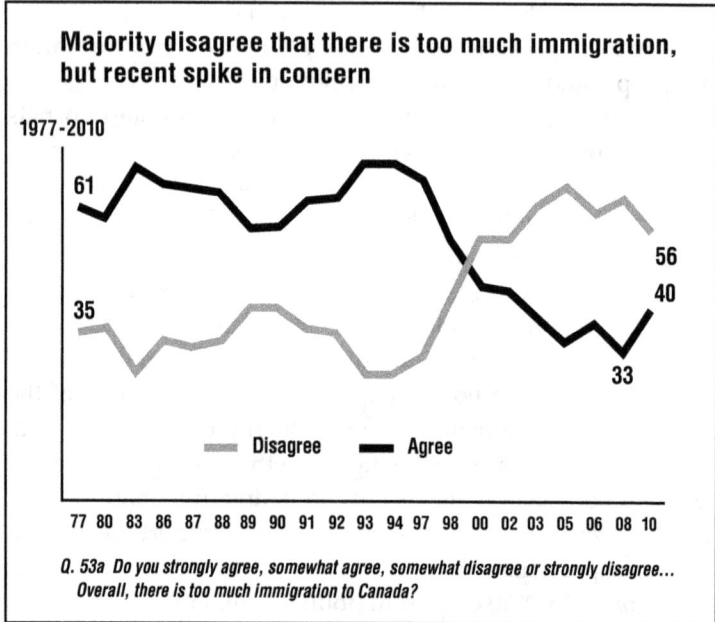

Q. 53a  Do you strongly agree, somewhat agree, somewhat disagree or strongly disagree...
Overall, there is too much immigration to Canada?

*Source: Michael Adams and Keith Neuman. 2011. "Canadian Immigration Policy, Citizenship & Demographic Diversity Review," Canadian Public Opinion – Focus Canada. Environics Institute, presented at the University of Ottawa on June 8.*

[36] A very good omen is that senior officials of the Canadian government have begun to speak candidly about some aspects of this sensitive and important issue. Immigration Minister Jason Kenney, while continuing to state very clearly, and rightly, that Canada profits when she admits skilled immigrants (blue-collar or white-collar), now clearly states also just under 20 percent of newcomers are primary economic immigrants; another 35 percent represents their spouse and children. To this 55 percent of the annual immigration flow is added another 10 to 13 percent who are admitted on humanitarian or compassionate grounds. This means that two-thirds of the annual intake consists of immigrants whose admission is relatively uncontroversial if the selection processes were adequate and not unduly lax. The question is the last third, of which half is made of non-economic parents and grandparents of newcomers. Minister Kenney told a House of Commons committee on

# A frontal attack on this wicked problem may be counterproductive

This issue domain is fraught with groundless beliefs manufactured over decades by *le pouvoir social*, naïve academics, irresponsible media and disingenuous politicians. As a result, experts have been notoriously unsuccessful or, at the very least, very slow in countervailing the general pro-immigration and multiculturalist narrative developed in Canada in the aftermath of the adoption of the Charter of Rights. It is my view that the present dynamic has taken such a hold on the Canadian scene that a frontal attack is bound to fail.[37]

Acting frontally would be too politically destabilizing since the new Harper government was elected in May 2011 with the support of 57.5 percent of the votes of foreign-born citizens and 54.1 percent of the votes of visible minorities.[38] It would be unwise for those impatient to see reforms in the immigration and refugee policies to believe that it is a crusade that the new government could easily be persuaded to support.

---

October 20, 2011 that family-class immigration has to be scaled back, "that there have to be practical limits to our generosity... based on our country's economic needs, our fiscal capacity." ("The problem with grandma," *National Post*, Editorial. October 22, 2011.) There would appear to be a growing newly-minted agreement that "too much non-economic immigration in a welfare state is a recipe for fiscal trouble." Such openly-acknowledged concerns might mean that the joint impact of tighter selection criteria (e.g., working knowledge of one of the official languages, better assessment of security and cultural fit), and scaling back family-class immigration and other non-economic immigration (except those admitted on humanitarian and compassionate grounds) might lead to a significant decline in the annual immigration flows to ensure that they are in keeping with Canada's absorptive capacity. A reduction of up to one-third of the annual flow might easily ensue.

[37] A measure of the resilience of the myth of the positive economic impact mass immigration might be that it has had toxic effects in many places that one would have regarded as naturally immune to such fantasies. I heard at the annual meeting of the Canadian Economics Association in June 2011 that the Conference Board of Canada has joined the phalanx of the believers, and that it now is developing scenarios of 350,000 and 450,000 new official immigrants per year for Canada.

[38] John Ibbitson. June 6, 2011. "Tories are rebels in search of a cause." *Globe & Mail*, A4.

What is required is an oblique approach: the recognition that, in the face of complex policy problems, an indirect route may prove the most effective.[39] This does not require that one lose track of the main challenges, but it demands that an awareness of the complexity of the environment be factored in – mental prisons, immigration industry powers, deep-rooted myths, political parties that are carried into competitive exaggeration on the immigration front, etc.

## Scheming virtuously on three fronts: a brief sketch

What I suggest is guerilla action: (1) destroying myths; (2) proposing practical ways to manage tractable administrative problems that could be dealt with without political fallout, and might serve as a Trojan horse to accomplish the goal of reducing the massive and indiscriminate immigration flows; and (3) working at developing a social movement in favour of a wiser and more prudent immigration and refugee regime.

On the first front, analytical and critical thinking is the *sine qua non*. The study of the Quebec scene by Dubreuil and Marois[40] might be regarded as a model. It has exposed the myths of the major economic benefits and the demographically corrective power of immigration. Its findings were widely reported in the mainstream media because the work was not perceived as advocacy, but as myth-busting. They have also added a few case studies showing the immense flaws in the operations of the current immigration regime as a source of waste and flagrant ineffectiveness in certain precise areas (e.g., the immigrant investor program). The clarity and detached tone of their work has attracted the attention of the mainstream media that usually ignore strident frontal attacks on the conventional wisdom. Much material available in the

---

[39] John Kay. 2011. *Obliquity – Why our goals are best achieved indirectly*. London: Profile Books.
[40] Benoît Dubreuil and Guillaume Marois, 2011.

literature could be used in this manner to undermine the foundations of other such myths now in good currency.

On the second front, what is needed is a very precise and detailed *cahier de doléances*, explicitly defining the Kafkaesque dimensions of the immigration policy regime as it operates now and putting forward very detailed, precise and practical propositions to correct these flaws. In all cases, such as the modification of the flawed screening and selection of immigrants (as well as other such mechanisms), the corrective proposals must be formulated in a manner that shows them to be technically feasible, socially acceptable, implementable, and not too politically destabilizing.[41]

Many such changes may be effected without much fanfare and could make a significant difference. A provisional list of key points that deserve special attention might be:

- a tighter selection process for highly-skilled workers in occupations in high demand to ensure that the expertise of the newcomer is effectively relevant;
- a requirement for face-to-face interviews of all applicants by visa officers;
- more emphasis on the prior knowledge of French and English;
- limitations to be imposed on family class and chain immigration; and,
- discontinuing visas to professionals who have not met Canadian standards.

Work on this second front is not likely to progress if the conversation remains at the level of evasive thinking and vague complaints. What is required here is a re-engineering of the administration and governance of the immigration and refugee policy regimes. One cannot expect reasonable practical solutions to be proposed by well-meaning but ill-informed bystanders. This is a front on which the technical

---

[41] Carl Taylor. 1997. "The ACIDD Test: A Framework for Policy Planning and Decision-Making," *Optimum*, 27(4): 53-56.

expertise of personnel with direct experience of these processes will be required.[42]

The tactical interventions at the administrative level must be based on grievous flaws in the operational process that most citizens can readily understand, appreciate and denounce. Among the concerns that may strike a sensitive chord are:

- security and health concerns;
- observed reluctance to integrate that challenges the Canadian *ethos*;
- growing ghettoization in Canada;
- growing difficulties of integration as new cohorts fare worse and worse;
- radicalization of young immigrants in Canada;
- threats to the social fabric; and,
- threats to the welfare state.

On the third front, the task is the organization and the fostering of emergent publics – calling attention to problems of social importance and fostering discussion and debates about immigration and diversity. This is the task of public intellectuals – to create new forums, to bring new actors onto the scene, and to "make questionable what has previously not been questioned and thereby open up larger areas of social life to public discussion, decision, and action."[43]

This construction task is of necessity Himalayan. It means engaging in an exercise to seriously attenuate the

---

[42] For a more detailed discussion of these administrative pathologies and ways to correct them, see James Bissett in Herbert Grubel (ed.), 2009. In particular, it will be interesting to see if the recent Supreme Court of Canada decision (about Canadian sponsors of immigrating family members who have agreed to support these newcomers for the first three years having to reimburse governments for expenditures incurred and benefits received by the sponsored party) will generate a humane but forceful pressure for such reimbursement, or if this legitimate claim will not be seriously enforced. The nature of the response may or may not have a significant impact on the flow of sponsored immigrants.

[43] Ian Angus. 2001. *Emergent Publics*. Winnipeg: Arbeiter Ring Publishing, p. 65; also Gilles Paquet. 2009. *Scheming virtuously: the road to collaborative governance*. Ottawa: Invenire, conclusion.

cognitive dissonance in this issue domain, to bring to light assumptions the group is not aware it is making, and to transform the norms in good currency and the reference points, so as to align them better with what would be both a sounder appreciation of the environment and a lesser degree of false consciousness.

This is a longer term project. One cannot change a culture overnight, or correct the distortions that have been decades in the making. The project also needs to build on a position that is both strategically **offensive** in aiming to discredit the prevailing ideology, but also strategically **inclusive** in finding ways to appeal to all reasonable persons capable of critical thinking.

## Conclusion

This approach may be seen as too prudent and too timid for a situation that many perceive to be a looming major disaster for Canada – an irreversible loss of control of its destiny – as the percentage of foreign-born Canadians continues to increase, accompanied by accelerated immigration rates, a surreptitious erosion of the common public culture, and stubborn and irresponsible denial in the face of all the signs that there is cause for concern with the present immigration and refugee regimes. Yet, given the mortgage of disinformation and deception over the last 25 years, and the consequent identity redefinition, this may be the only way. A more aggressive approach is likely to backfire.

In the short run, the Trojan horse approach appears to be the most promising strategy. Tinkering with the selection process and all the technical apparatus of the immigration and refugees regimes to make them more meaningful and effective would undoubtedly lead to a reduction in the immigration flows without much fanfare. The cultural change in the long run has to do with consciousness-raising, nurturing emergent publics, and engaging in a redefinition of identity. This is not an easy task, and it will take time.

# CHAPTER 2

# | Immigration and the Solidarity-Diversity-Security Nexus

"Canada has no national culture..."
– *Sheila Finestone, Secretary of State for Multiculturalism, 1995*

## Introduction

Nothing can be more telling about the Canadian intelligentsia's state of *insouciance* than the cancellation (for lack of interest) of a conference on diversity and security that was planned for September 2010 – at the very time when security concerns were omnipresent in daily conversations in the forum, and when the link to diversity and immigration was being explicitly argued. It would appear that dealing with the diversity-security nexus remains a taboo topic, even more than the diversity-solidarity issue. Yet these issues are of great concern to Canadians and need to be publicly addressed.

A most important mental prison that works at preventing such debates is the dogma propounded by some influential Canadian academics and ideologues (the two sets intersect) that these issues have been permanently settled, that there is a 'national consensus'[44] on indiscriminate and massive

---

[44] Peter O'Neil. September 25, 2010. "Is Canada Up to the Immigration Challenge?" *Ottawa Citizen*, A6.

immigration, and on the fact that it has no impact on solidarity and security in Canada. In fact, there is no such national consensus. The objective of this chapter is to question the foundations of this specious argument.

First, I clarify the meaning of these interfaces, and show that the presumption that diversity will not reduce solidarity and security is ill-founded. Second, I suggest that the current Canadian immigration and refugee system is in need of repairs both on the quantitative front (not stopping immigration flows but regulating them), and on the qualitative front (through more effective selection and integration mechanisms) in the name of a strengthened notion of citizenship. A pan-Canadian conversation on these issues is urgently required.

## The SDS nexus

### Fraternity as linchpin

Tackling all the implications of trade-offs among solidarity, diversity and security (SDS) is all but impossible in a short chapter. Consequently, I have chosen to focus on an approach that puts front and centre the notion of **fraternity** as a linchpin in this nexus of issues. Therefore, my argument has a Henri Bergson flavour. For him, fraternity is the oil that makes the gears of equality and liberty mesh as smoothly as possible. Without a sense of fraternity (trust in and affection for our co-citizens), liberty tends to become a toxic absolute that can lead to radical inequalities, and equality can become a justification for severe limitations of freedom.[45]

Despite the angelic pronouncements of a variety of academics and ideologues, fraternity is eroded by diversity, and policies like multiculturalism (that purport to strengthen the boundaries between persons and among groups in a propulsive way) can have only a negative impact on solidarity and, *ceteris paribus*, tend to increase security risks.

---

[45] This is a point raised by Raymond D. Boisvert. 2005. "Diversity as Fraternity Lite," *The Journal of Speculative Philosophy*, 19(2): 120-128; Henri Bergson. 1955. *Les deux sources de la morale et de la religion*. Paris: Presses Universitaires de France, p. 300.

**Practical reason** would suggest that there are limits to diversity – limits beyond which the cost/benefit ratio (whatever the method of calculation and the range of costs and benefits considered) tips over and fraternity becomes significantly eroded.[46] Thus, unless one can demonstrate that auxiliary arrangements are in place (tighter selection, better integration services, etc.) that can and will contain such risks, the **precautionary principle** would suggest that to proceed blindly toward such tipping points where costs become greater than benefits, and to ignore the potential malefits that may develop from diversity, is irresponsible.[47]

## Diversity

The word **diversity** has been used as a convenient label to connote very different realities and to underpin quite different action programs.

First, diversity has been used as a picturesque word to describe the outcome of the great worldwide shuffle of population that has led to much commingling of different cultural groups in many regions of the world – a result of the reduction of transportation costs and the lowering of territorial borders.

Second, it has also been used to connote the objective pursued by some countries (either wittingly or unwittingly, whether successfully or not) to increase such intercultural migrations in order either to recalibrate the age distribution in an ageing country, or to get access to a higher level of creativity and innovation through the greater social learning likely to ensue when different cultures and frames of reference are cross-pollinating.

Thirdly, the word has also been used to clinically identify the plight of countries torn apart or perceived as losing their soul as a result of either an unwelcome co-habitation of deeply

---

[46] Gilles Paquet and Paul Reid. 2004. "Are There Limits to Diversity?" *www. optimumonline*, 33(1): 13-19.

[47] François Ewald et al. 2001. *Le principe de précaution*. Paris: Presses Universitaires de France.

different and hostile groups within the same territory, or of an unbridled invasion of external groups becoming established as isolated communities in a host society and generating fractiousness and factions. In such cases, it is asserted that far from leading to more creativity and innovation, diversity is more likely to generate social enclaves, ensuing social friction, and higher costs of transaction.

Whatever the sense of the word, diversity is not an absolute social good. It may be a source of social energy, but it may also be a source of dissipation of social energy. The interaction with evolving contextual factors has made diversity more than a matter of nominal recognition, respect and tolerance of otherness. When converted into a policy, it has often translated into a tool that generates balkanization and group entitlements. As a result, diversity has sometimes become associated with the erosion of certain basic principles that the host society holds dear.

But the trade-offs diversity imposes on a society are not easily discussed. Indeed, the very notion of 'governance of diversity' (i.e., the intentional use of instruments to optimize diversity and to ensure that dangerous thresholds are not crossed) is challenged in many circles as politically incorrect and ethically wrong.

This is a remarkably obtuse point of view which defines diversity not as a matter of choice, but as a matter of fate. Refusing to govern the diversity interface has come to be blessed with the name of virtue in such circles, while any effort at attempting to manage the diversity of a society has been scorned as a misguided effort to limit it and is, therefore, chastised as a sign of latent fascism.

It is my view that the governance of diversity is the central challenge facing pluralistic societies, and that no responsible society should agree to be shaped by faceless external forces. The question is how do we do this job?

## Solidarity

As Raymond D. Boisvert puts it, "the triumvirate diversity, tolerance, multiculturalism, comes up short...when looked at from the perspective of fraternity."[48] Being solicitous of diversity risks generating silo-societies, tolerance emphasizes the negative leave-them-alone kind of virtue, and multiculturalism further works at maintaining and enhancing cultural differences (as a matter of policy). All this translates into enlarging intercultural gaps and generating relatively more isolated communities. It does not encourage genuine affiliation and active dialogue and, without such features, the sufficient conditions for fraternity to materialize cannot be expected to ensue.

One of the consequences of declaring diversity a primary good has been that, at times, it has been pursued to the detriment of other objectives, like freedom, efficiency, equality and the like.[49] Probably the most sensitive trade-off for those who claim to be 'progressive' is the one between diversity and solidarity. Since progressives are clearly of the opinion that both these goals are absolutely desirable, they would face a dilemma if it were to be discovered that the multicultural approach to diversity, for example, generates lower levels of social cohesion and solidarity, and might thereby undermine the egalitarianism-driven welfare state.

This question was explicitly raised by Brian Barry, and his book has generated a heated debate.[50] The main points in contention were aptly synthesized by David Goodhart in response to the more specific question, "is Britain becoming too diverse to sustain the mutual obligations that underpin a good society and a generous welfare state?"[51] The issue has since received a fair amount of attention, both nationally and internationally, and a synthesis of recent findings emerging

---

[48] Raymond D. Boisvert, 2005, p. 120.

[49] The rest of this section draws freely from Gilles Paquet. 2008. *Deep Cultural Diversity – A Governance Challenge*. Ottawa: University of Ottawa Press, p. 78ff.

[50] Brian Barry. 2001. *Culture and Equality: An Egalitarian Critique of Multiculturalism*. Cambridge, MA: Harvard University Press.

[51] David Goodhart. February 2004. "Too Diverse?" *Prospect Magazine*, issue 95.

from the work done by a consortium of Canadian researchers has been prepared by Keith Banting.[52] The nuanced Banting summary directly tackled the two central questions: are there deep tensions at work between heterogeneity and redistribution, and between recognition and redistribution?

The results pertaining to the first question are that "there is no evidence ... that countries with large immigrant populations have greater difficulty in sustaining and enhancing their historic welfare commitments. But large increases in the foreign-born population do seem to matter."[53]

As for the second and much more difficult question (as to whether explicit recognition policies like official multiculturalism tend to weaken redistribution), there seems to be no support for it as a bald claim, but Banting admits that "there are more localized circumstances where particular forms of recognition erode particular forms of redistribution."[54]

Interest in the issue reached a climax in 2007 with the publication of Robert Putnam's *E Pluribus Unum*.[55] This paper, based on a study of over 30,000 people, and over 40 communities, comes to the clear conclusion that, after standardizing on all sorts of extraneous factors, more diversity means lower social capital; and, that diversity, at least in the short run, seems to entail less social cohesion – less volunteer work, less charity, less involvement, less belief that the citizen can make a difference.

Given the time lag that might be involved in the generation and disappearance of such tensions, the empirical work on these difficult questions leaves them unresolved in any definitive way in the long run. But it is quite difficult to believe – given the extraordinary resistance to any symbolic recognition (like distinct society) and the general apprehension generated by the slogan "different but equal"

[52] Keith G. Banting. 2007. "Canada as Counter Narrative," *www.optimumonline.ca*, 37(3): 2-15

[53] Keith G. Banting, 2007, p. 7.

[54] Keith G. Banting, 2007, p. 10.

[55] Robert D. Putnam. 2007. "E Pluribus Unum: Diversity and Community in the 21st Century," *Scandinavian Political Studies*, 30(2): 137-174.

– that an increase in symbolic recognition (and therefore in separateness) does not reduce solidarity.

Indeed, much anecdotal evidence would appear to reveal that the sharper and the more publicly celebrated the symbolic recognition of separateness (as in the case of French Canadians and the Aboriginals), the more the sense of belonging and trust is eroded.[56] One can choose to ascribe such antagonism to history or to other institutional and policy contexts (as it is often done – whatever this may mean), but it is simplistic to discard encouraged separateness as a root cause. And it is clear that if recognition and separateness are clearly encouraged by a multicultural policy, then that policy can only generate a weakening of the social fabric over the long haul. How can the encouragement to remain apart be expected to generate anything different?

The worst aspect of the formalization and 'judiciarization' of these differences that the multiculturalism policy encourages (and the parallel insistence that there is no such thing as Canadian culture, or that it is at best very 'thin') is that it fosters a certain civic *malaise* as these phenomena shape a certain way for minorities and immigrant groups to think about themselves, and leads them to emphasize their differences, to play the 'humiliation card' when such differences are not honoured, and to demand more initiatives to recognize the equality of cultures.

Indeed, one of the dirty little secrets nobody wishes to face is that the virtuous circle of more solidarity generating more redistribution generating more solidarity may have been broken by way of the significant and relatively abrupt increases in diversity that strained the absorptive capacity of Canadian society. Any heightened recognition of separateness cannot but generate less solidarity (however much time it may take to be revealed in multiple regressions), and this can only

---

[56] Keith G. Banting et al. (eds.). 2007. *The Art of the State. Volume 3, Belonging?* Montreal: Institute for Research on Public Policy, conclusion; see also Bonnie H. Erickson. 2007. "Ties that bind and ties that divide" in Banting et al. (eds.), p. 601-609.

translate into less willingness to take part in egalitarian inter-cultural redistribution.

The debates around the trade-off between diversity/ multiculturalism and solidarity have been haunted by the spectre of egalitarianism. Since egalitarianism is a canonical reference in progressive circles, and this reference is non-negotiable, no trade-off is possible with the other absolute – identity and recognition of separateness. To get out of this dilemma, one has to assume that not only is there no need for any trade-off between these absolutes, but that they necessarily go hand in hand. Indeed, the conclusion of the Banting 2007 volume ends up with a re-affirmation that the search for equality is the road to intercultural peace and prosperity.[57]

A more reasonable way to envisage the dilemma is to debunk the idea of the sacred absolute character of egalitarianism and to replace it by a weaker and softer notion likely to lend itself to trade-offs. Equability may be a more useful reference.

This word – **equability** – is a term that Merriam-Webster defines as "lack of noticeable, unpleasant, or extreme variation or inequality."[58] Equability would appear to capture well the sort of balancing act required in the practical search for openness, inclusiveness and high-performance. Yet, this is a word that is not in good currency in Canada where terms like "entitlements" and "egalitarianism" – words that are much more legalistic and speak of non-negotiability – are the sort of reference points most often quoted.

The use of equability would shift the doctrinaire position of the progressive from an either-or to a more-or-less framework.

Instead of staunchly denying any possibility of trade-off between equality and diversity, the word equability would foster a discussion in which both terms are open to some accommodation. This would pose the challenge of defining

[57] This is argued despite the fact that interregional and intergroup laundering of money and other redistribution schemes have ceased, for quite a long time, to be able to claim that they are at the source of national solidarity (if they ever were), except in the sermons of the progressives, for whom it is an article of faith.

[58] Merriam-Webster Online, www.merriam-webster.com.

how much egalitarianism needs to be abandoned in order to accommodate a so-called requisite, but not absolute, degree of separateness and recognition. Equability would raise the possibility of acceptable inequalities. On the other side, the notion of recognition would also have to give and become less of an absolute.

Consequently, it may not be possible to proceed further without also some relativization of what multiculturalism has tended to make absolute.

## Security

Security – the other word in this triad – is a weasel word. It connotes a wide variety of phenomena ranging from physical safety from violence as the result of a general agreement on rules of behaviour in a particular society, to a psychological sense that one is protected from hostile occurrences that may threaten the full use of agency. In general, it refers to the degree of protection (real or assumed) against danger, damage, etc.

The adjective 'secure' is usually attached either to an environment that is deemed non-threatening or providing a zone of protection, or to the state of mind of individuals or groups that have developed a sense (real or assumed) that they are thereby liberated from threats that would prevent them from making the highest and best use of all their assets (physical, intellectual, spiritual, emotional, etc.). The sense of security is associated in good part with the sentiment of being protected from a hostile environment by a sort of 'we-community,' or latent reciprocity, that serves as a shield or insurance against threats, or at least against the malefits attached to such threats.

Because of the *mélange* of objective and subjective characteristics of security, it is not easy to get agreement on indices that would measure security in a manner that would gain a consensus on their usefulness and reliability. The issue is thorny because there are, at times, important gaps between official measures that sound reassuring (about criminality, for instance) and the state of mind of a population that is exposed daily to violence in the street. Moreover, the meaning of the word is considerably affected, depending on what terrains are felt to be in need of security (border, infrastructure, public health, criminal activities, etc.) and whose security one is concerned with (the state, society, human lives, etc.).

Obviously, there is no way to provide absolute protection from the vagaries of the environment (natural disasters, economic instability, terrorism, etc.), but solidarity provides protective devices that enable an individual to better weather the storm with the help of co-citizens as a result of some sort of guarantee or insurance. To the extent that any expression of kinship or sense of belonging (we-feeling) is eroded, solidarity is bound to be eroded, and the willingness to provide common protection against the bad circumstances in one's environment is also eroded.

This has been observed and commented on as the European Union expanded. The growing diversity made it more difficult to develop a perception of commonality, and solidarity has become more elusive.[59] Consequently, mutual support (in the sense of contingent assistance, provision of social goods, and sharing of the financial burden to ensure less insecurity for other members of the 'community') has diminished.

Therefore, it is not surprising that massive and indiscriminate immigration might be generating some erosion of solidarity, and erosion of a sense of security, through its generation of a significant and relatively abrupt increase in diversity that might affect the sense of kinship or commonality.

But even though the current arrangements for dealing with immigration and refugees (arrived at by happenstance) are neither optimal nor even adequate, in a modern democratic society like Canada, it has nevertheless become a dogma in Canadian progressive circles to say that massive and indiscriminate immigration does not reduce solidarity and, therefore, does not increase security risks.[60]

[59] Ines Hartwig and Phedon Nicolaides. 2003. "Elusive Solidarity in an Enlarged European Union," *Eipascope*, (3): 19-25.

[60] This is a dogma that more dispassionate experts condemn (e.g., see Jeffrey G. Reitz. July-August 2010. "Getting Past Yes or No," *Literary Review of Canada*, p. 3-4).

## Intellectual complacency and sophistry

As Jeffrey Reitz suggests, complacency is not what might be expected from policy analysis. So the prevailing view that the existing arrangements about immigration and refugees are optimal – and that the burden of the proof is squarely and entirely on the shoulders of those who are not satisfied with the status quo – makes it eminently easy to automatically dismiss in a facile way the complaints of those who testify that the current flawed arrangements have led them to experience "diffuse anxiety."[61] This is hardly satisfactory. Indeed, the view that, until the requisite regression analyses have 'proved' beyond a reasonable doubt that the existing regime and policies are destructive, they should continue to be regarded as optimal, is not a prudent way to deal with policies. Yet this has been the canonical position adopted by the so-called progressive intelligentsia and their advocacy friends.

There is a substantial amount of evidence that suggests that the Canadian immigration system is not working well.[62] I noted in chapter 1 the many naked facts that point to an immigration and refugee system that requires a revision in depth. These facts go a long way toward explaining why, with each new cohort of immigrants over the last 30 years, the level of relative earnings of newcomers has fallen increasingly behind those levels achieved by those born in Canada – as Patrick Grady graphically demonstrated (figure 3) in his submission to the Stakeholder and Public Consultation on Immigration Levels and Mix in September 2011.[63]

This relative deterioration of the fate of newcomers over the last while is a most important indicator of both the inadequacy of the appreciation of Canada's absorptive capacity, and of the selection criteria and the integration mechanisms in good

---

[61] Phil Ryan. 2009. *Multicultiphobia*. Toronto: University of Toronto Press.
[62] Don Drummond and Francis Fong. 2010. "An economics perspective on Canadian immigration," *Policy Options*, 31(7): 28-34.
[63] Patrick Grady. September 2011. *Immigration is Too High and Not Based on Canada's Economic Interests: A Submission to the Stakeholder and Public Consultation on Immigration Levels and Mix.* www.immigrationreform.ca; Don Drummond and Francis Fong, 2010, p. 30.

currency – that is, evidence that the flow and composition of newcomers are not in keeping with what a sound evaluation of absorptive capacity would warrant.

Growing concern about increasing ghettoization, dual loyalties, cultural relativism, the explicit expression of disdain by newcomers for the cultural majority, radicalization in Canada of immigrants from other countries, etc., is also palpable and too readily discarded as anecdotal evidence. Meanwhile, the weakest of arguments supporting those in whose view Canada is doing quite well in the integration of ethnic minorities, and their claim that a significant increase in immigration would have no negative impacts (whatever negative impacts there are being ascribed to "institutional and policy contexts") are receiving the most uncritical acclaim.[64]

## FIGURE 3:
## Recent immigrant to Canadian-born earnings ratio

| Years | with university degree | | with no university degree | |
|-------|------------------------|---------|---------------------------|---------|
|       | **Males** | **Females** | **Males** | **Females** |
| 1980 | 0.77 | 0.59 | 0.84 | 0.86 |
| 1990 | 0.63 | 0.63 | 0.67 | 0.77 |
| 2000 | 0.58 | 0.52 | 0.65 | 0.66 |
| 2005 | 0.48 | 0.43 | 0.61 | 0.56 |

*Source: Statistics Canada, censuses of population 1982, 1991, 2001 and 2006.*

---

[64] What would be quite revealing is a critical analysis of the increasingly nuanced discourse of Will Kymlicka, or a less uncritical examination of the weak foundations of some of Irene Bloemraad's argument about the meaning of citizenship acquisition, or about the real meaning of some of the intricate regression results presented by Christel Kesler and Irene Bloemraad. 2010. "Does Immigration Erode Social Capital?" *Canadian Journal of Political Science*, 43(2): 319-347, from which it is inferred skillfully that "institutional and policy contexts" are to be indicted for any malefits and not significant immigration and increase in diversity.

## Citizenship and the SDS nexus

Canadian immigration policies have evolved over time, but they consistently echoed a concern about **absorptive capacity** until the beginning of the 1990s, when Canada appeared to have abandoned any such concern and failed to cut back on immigration flows, despite major labour market woes at the time. Moreover, there seems to have been an important *insouciance* about the lack of careful selection of immigrants, even though this careful screening may have been a major source of earlier successes of the immigration strategy.

### Too elusive a notion of citizenship

Concerns about absorptive capacity, the growing difficulties of integration of newcomers, and the need for newcomers to adapt to the Canadian way of life have been merrily ignored and remained not discussed at the official level for much of the last decades. This has been the case despite a Dominion Institute survey, conducted by the Innovative Research Group, which suggested that, in 2005, 70 percent of Canadians indicated that adapting to the Canadian way of life should be the top priority of newcomers.[65]

Immigrants to a country (unless they plan to stay only temporarily) request the privilege of becoming a 'sort of kin' as citizen (i.e., as co-producers of governance in a pluralist polity). Consequently, the sort of immigration and refugee regimes that can be regarded as satisfactory will have to be gauged on the basis of the notion of citizenship that is agreed to, and absorptive capacity (and the speed at which the absorption can proceed) gauged accordingly.

Some see citizenship as sheer legal status, others as participation in governance, and still others as belonging. These ideal-types may be represented as the apexes of a triangle.[66]

---

[65] Quoted in the Policy Research Initiative's program on cultural diversity (*Multicultural Canada in the 21st Century: Harnessing Opportunities and Managing Pressures*).

[66] The following paragraphs draw freely from Gilles Paquet, 2008, chapter 5.

At one apex of this citizenship triangle is the liberal idea of citizenship rooted in the notion of legal status – a 'thin' notion that is in good currency in the Anglo-Saxon world. Here, citizenship inheres in individuals, who are seen as the bearers of rights, and it is couched in a language of entitlements. Citizens do not have to do anything, or at least not much, to become or remain citizens. It minimizes participation requirements and expects little sense of identification. This liberal notion emphasizes the centrality of negative freedom (i.e., protection against interference with individual choices by the state).

At a second apex is the civic republican view of citizenship. It is largely couched in terms of duties and defines citizenship as a notion with a high valence given to practice and participation – the citizen is a producer of governance. It calls on individuals to become members of the community, to participate in the culture and governance of the community. This concept emphasizes positive freedom (i.e., the person's ability to do this or that, and the duty to help others in that respect).

A third apex emphasizes neither status nor participation, but the process of belonging. In this zone of the triangle, of central importance are the recognition, respect and esteem given to the individual and his circumstances.

Citizenship may cover a whole range of possible meanings, with all sorts of mixed cases giving different weights to each of these dimensions. Moreover, instead of being absorbed into a simple, formal and legal linkage between the citizen and the state, citizenship relationships have evolved into a looser, but more encompassing, covenant covering a web of relationships among members of the community.

The proliferation of multiple citizenships has heightened the complexity of these arrangements as in the case of persons or organizations purporting to hold membership in many clubs at the same time. This has led both to ugly abuses of power (when a group of citizens has been branded by a paranoid state as likely to collaborate with the enemy, as happened to Japanese Canadians during World War II), but also to individuals and organizations using their 'citizenship of convenience' to take opportunistic advantage of all possible entitlements in the *pays d'adoption*, while shirking all the responsibilities of citizenship in the same naïvely tolerant host country. Many have complained that Canadian citizenship has been somewhat trivialized, both by systematically diluting the conditions imposed on its acquisition and maintenance, and by allowing multiple citizenships to further dilute any sense that there must be loyalty and responsibilities attached to the citizen's burden of office.[67]

Canadians as individuals are inclined to be both much more demanding in their definition of citizenship than Canadian officials, and much more willing than bureaucrats and politicians to craft *de facto* **workable terms of integration**. They define it not only in terms of a bundle of rights and liberties, but also in terms of responsibilities, attitudes, sensitivities and identities.

However, public officials boast of having no concern about defining any such set of expectations in terms of integration for newcomers, on the grounds that one cannot ask anything from newcomers that one does not require explicitly from the native born. Making any additional demands from newcomers is automatically branded as intolerance, chauvinism or racism. As a matter of consequence, officials are also not very concerned with ensuring that newcomers are provided with the requisite help to become capable of participating fully in the host society. They even seem to feel that they have no legitimate basis for refusing to modify Canadian ways, in response to requests by newcomers claiming that such ways constitute a discriminatory stance against them. These bizarre views are held despite Canadians' having clearly stated their disagreement with such views, and despite Canadians' strong beliefs that newcomers should qualify before being admitted to the host society, and that it is a priority commitment expected from newcomers that they will adapt to the Canadian ways.

This official position is quite treacherous: *de facto* terms of integration are bound to evolve as expectations and

---

[67] Martin Collacott. 2008. "Has it become too easy to acquire Canadian citizenship?" *Canadian Diversity*, 6(4): 141-144.

environments change, and there may be a need for arbitration between newcomers' demands and the limits to the tolerance of the host society. This is the fundamental challenge that Canadian leaders have refused to confront.[68]

The current official Canadian refusal to engage in an exercise of definition of the terms of integration is an irresponsible stance that is not inconsequential for Canadian society. The lack of a

[68] The media have actively supported this insouciant attitude of the officials and the intelligentsia about integration. Indeed, they have openly denounced in editorials and in so-called 'factual reporting' efforts to help newcomers to develop a better sense of the sensitivities of the host population. A recent initiative of the City of Gatineau was to prepare such a guide (Gatineau, 2011. *Énoncé de valeurs – des clés pour mon intégration à Gatineau*), which elicited scorn on the front page of the *Globe & Mail* (December 5, 2011) and in the editorial page of the *Ottawa Citizen* (December 6, 2011), and has been denounced as demeaning. The fact that the guide was prepared by a Haiti-born city councillor who has lived in the area for decades and, therefore, by someone who would be knowledgeable about what might be useful to newcomers, had no impact on the English Canadian newspapers for which political correctness has become such a mental prison that a gesture of courtesy to help newcomers has been transmogrified into patronizing and demeaning contempt for newcomers. It would appear that, in those English Canadian media, efforts to make newcomers aware of certain sensitivities of the host society is reprehensible and politically incorrect, even if it might be useful to newcomers. One has a sense that reasonable accommodation in those circles has to occur without the benefit of a conversation – a conversation about how we have decided to live together in this country would appear to be as taboo a topic as sex was in the Victorian age. It is fascinating to compare how this bizarre sense of outrage had no echoes in French Canada. Could it be that cultural relativism has taken such a hold on English Canadian intelligentsia and media that making newcomers aware of our ways of *vivre-ensemble* and of our sensitivities is regarded as unacceptable? Fortunately, hundreds of emails received by these newspapers have shown that English Canadians are not as silly as their newspapers. None of these responses, recorded on the Internet, were published in the paper versions of the newspapers. The intelligentsia and the media would appear to buy the doctrine that it is inappropriate to make newcomers aware of the common public culture and of our sense of *savoir-vivre*. This is an extraordinary example of making newcomers aware of our own culture being denounced in the name of a priority having to be granted to not offend those who are asking to join our own society and may not share our norms. Some would say it pushes self-deprecation to absurd limits. Yet, the officialdom of the City of Gatineau withdrew the document after the complaint of one immigrant who objected to it: officialdom at the municipal level shamefully betrayed its burden of office in facilitating the integration of newcomers to placate the high priests of political correctness. This is nothing to be proud of, but it is quite revealing.

clear notion of the responsibilities attached to citizenship can only lead to fuzziness in the definition of the limits of tolerance that can legitimately be expected by newcomers. More than any other factor, the very reluctance of the Canadian government to foster debates leading to a clear articulation of guideposts is probably the main source of concern for those who favour tighter controls on immigration to Canada, because the current regimes appear to foster an 'anything goes' attitude.

The danger of this unwillingness to establish clear conditions of admission and terms of integration is that it has eroded trust. Significant groups have found it opportune to take advantage of Canadian benefits without accepting any of the obligations that constitute the flip side of this moral contract of citizenship. In the longer run, this sort of abuse can only lead to action generating greater exclusion than would otherwise be desirable. Both old and new Canadians are consequently bound to be worse off.

For the Canadian citizen (as opposed to Canadian officialdom and intelligentsia), citizenship is a privilege and newcomers must qualify for it. Moreover, a citizen is granted rights so as to enable him/her to meet his/her responsibilities, his/her burden of office as a citizen. This burden of office entails active participation in the polity in transforming disruptive differences into liveable relations. The citizen (old and new) is therefore expected to be actively involved in a pluralistic society, in transforming a community of fate into a repertoire of established ways of dealing with conflicts, both actual and potential, and in arriving, in the case of the newcomer, through internalizing the sensitivities of the host society at a shared definition of acceptable results.[69]

### Impact of massive and indiscriminate immigration

Dealing with such a high volume of immigrants has created problems for their screening. The Office of the Auditor General

[69] Herman R. van Gunsteren. 1998. *A Theory of Citizenship*. Boulder: Westview Press.

(OAG) has explicitly questioned the officials' capacity to maintain the quality of decisions and the integrity of the program, and has noted serious deficiencies in the way admissibility criteria related to health, criminality and security have been applied throughout the 1990s. The OAG has also complained about the limited progress made despite repeated warnings.[70]

Even very modest and commonsensical modifications to the immigration policy, like insisting that immigrants have a basic working knowledge of one of the official languages before they arrive in Canada (something recommended by the Immigration Legislative Review and supported by 75 percent of the Canadian born and 73 percent of immigrants themselves according to a Vancouver poll) were successfully opposed by opposition parties, immigration activists and immigrant service organizations.[71]

Indeed, even the well-documented evidence of Canada's inadequate response to terrorism in controlling the entry and departure of non-Canadians into and from Canada's territory has failed to generate any meaningful reaction.[72]

Things are no better on the refugee policy front.

Although, inexplicably, there is a very high percentage of refugee claimants being accepted by Canada (three times the average rate of other refugee-receiving countries), little has been done: (1) to scrutinize the reasons for this; (2) to determine whether it constitutes a flow of refugees that is desirable, given the state of the socio-economy; and, (3) to establish whether the nature of this flow of refugees emerging from almost anywhere (as opposed to originating from UN-sponsored refugee camps) is indeed the best way to exercise our humanitarian concerns.

Even modest efforts to deal more effectively with the refugee smugglers have met with denunciations in progressive circles. They have also elicited threats of Charter-based court challenges from the advocacy group, Canadian Council for

---

[70] Martin Collacott. 2003. *Canada's Immigration Policy: The Need for Major Reform.* Vancouver: The Fraser Institute, p. 26-33.

[71] Martin Collacott, 2003, p. 37ff.

[72] Martin Collacott. 2006. *Canada's Inadequate Response to Terrorism: The Need for Policy Reform.* Vancouver: The Fraser Institute.

Refugees, for the perceived attempt to stream refugees (regular and irregular) in order to better deal with legitimate and illegitimate refugees.[73]

A confederacy of interest groups (political and non-political) appears to be determined (with much self-righteous fanfare) to prevent any attempts at correcting a system that all would concede, in private, is significantly flawed.

## The costs of inaction

A most important impediment to a meaningful discussion of the current immigration and refugee regimes is the lack of any reasonably accurate measure of the various costs to Canadians. These costs have been significant in the last two decades and they are likely to grow as more and more newcomers face more difficult circumstances and, consequently, downward trends in immigrant employment and earnings.[74]

These public costs are all the more invidious to the extent that they are indirectly borne not by the federal government that makes the major decisions about immigration flows, but by provincial and municipal governments that are saddled with the welfare costs of this increasingly impoverished group.

Some of these are the direct cash costs of handling the cases, associated with the benefits granted to immigrants and refugees and with the privileges granted to them (e.g., when, under the family re-unification programs, they can bring to Canada a number of relatives who may have no meaningful qualifications, nor any of the usually required linguistic capabilities). Over and beyond the direct cash outlays on these aspects of the cases, one must also factor in the indirect, spill-over social costs associated with the inadequate screening of newcomers, which leads to the additional costs associated with increased problems of health, criminality or terrorism.

Certain costs associated with certain segments of the administrative processes in those regimes are more easily

[73] Douglas Quand and Norma Greenaway. October 21, 2010. "Tories target refugee smugglers," *Ottawa Citizen*, A4.

[74] Jeffrey G. Reitz. 2000. *Immigrant Success in the Knowledge Economy*. Toronto: University of Toronto.

calculable and have been approximated. Government officials have stated that false refugee claimants cost Canadian taxpayers an average of $50,000. But most of the costs referred to in the previous paragraph have not been gauged, or even approximated. As a result, one has to rely on broad 'guesstimates' that are not at all re-assuring. Herbert Grubel has estimated that the benefits received by newcomers who have come to Canada in the last two decades (another segment of the total costs) are in the order of tens of billions of dollars per year in excess of what they pay in taxes.[75]

Most important, but also most difficult to measure, are the broad indirect social costs associated with the impact of significant increases in immigration and diversity on social capital, solidarity and security. Robert Putnam's 2007 study clearly stated that a significant increase in immigration tends to reduce solidarity and social capital.

Putnam's work has been attacked by those who regard diversity, and massive and indiscriminate immigration, as absolute goods. Much sophistry has been used in questioning Putnam's results, and in trying to ascribe whatever malefit is observed to other 'mediating' sources.[76] Yet, despite much massaging of data, the incontrovertible result of operating flawed regimes is a price tag that may not be totally clear, but is significant.

The same may be said about the costs of inaction in the face of the blossoming of processes of radicalization of immigrant groups *in situ* by networks and organizations operating in Canada with financial support from foreign countries. The funding of many Canadian mosques by Saudi Arabia (and the radicalization of Canadian residents in such loci) may be regarded as a well-documented case in point.[77]

[75] Herbert Grubel. 2005. "Immigration and the Welfare State in Canada: Growing Conflicts, Constructive Solutions," *Public Policy Sources*, no. 84. Vancouver: The Fraser Institute.

[76] Barbara Arneil. 2006. *Diverse Communities: The Problem with Social Capital.* Cambridge: Cambridge University Press.

[77] Global Futures Forum. 2006. "Radicalization, Violence and the Power of Networks." Report of the Autumn 2006 Brussels Workshop, www.thegff.com.

The external costs of such activities, and the impact they are bound to have on solidarity and security risks in Canada, are important: as Charles Taylor says, "solidarity is essential to democratic societies, otherwise they fall apart."[78]

Many of these malefits, borne by a society with a less intense solidarity, are undoubtedly at the basis of the 'diffuse anxiety' that permeates the Canadian population, but this is readily dismissed by the supporters of diversity and massive immigration. The fact that these costs have been generally occluded, and that any general discussion of these issues has been actively discouraged (when not openly condemned as politically incorrect), cannot hide the fact that all those 'costs' are real.

## Conclusion

However commonsensical the above criticisms may sound, they do not fit well with the official views underpinning the current immigration and refugee regimes. The dogma of mass and indiscriminate immigration prevails and the importance of protecting the common public culture is being ignored. Indeed, the progressive ideology has attacked any attempt at regulating immigration flows, or at screening newcomers in the name of protecting the common public culture, as nativist and racist.

Moreover, once such massive and indiscriminate immigration has generated the predictable pressures on the common public culture, and new demands for accommodation, the same progressive ideologues have argued that the host society should indeed fully accommodate these demands whatever the effects on the common public culture.

When signs of strain have shown that solidarity may be under stress, and that security risks may be on the increase, these signs have been ignored or declared ill-founded alarmism.

The very discourse that has attempted to draw attention to the legitimacy of protecting the common public culture (on the road to a more cosmopolitan common public culture

[78] Charles Taylor. September 30, 2010. "All for one and one for all," *The Globe & Mail*.

of the future)[79] has been denounced by multiculturalist ideologues, who wrongly and dangerously presume that because individuals must be regarded as equal, cultures must also be regarded as equal. Indeed, this fantasy of declaring all cultures equal has amounted to granting the same status both to the common public culture of societies that have evolved dramatically and painfully over the last many centuries and to those whose development, for all sorts of reasons, was arrested centuries ago. In that world of moral relativism, every move that can be interpreted as increasing diversity is automatically celebrated, even when it might entail an evolved liberal common public culture being infected by regressive mores.

Thus, hypertolerance (mostly in fear of the 'political correctness' police) has been elevated to the status of virtue, when, in fact, it reveals a grievous incapacity to critically appraise meaningful differences – a new version of voluntary servitude to moral relativism. This has become such an incredible force in the last few decades that nothing less than a Cassandra-like denunciation has any chance to attract the necessary attention and to result in any significant change.

As a result of this lack of critical thinking and moral fortitude in the face of the common public culture being undermined, one can reasonably be concerned about the possibility here of a quiet cultural capitulation as has been seen in societies with undefended common public cultures.

[79] This is the position defended in Gilles Paquet, 2008.

CHAPTER 3

# | Toward Fair Play and Hospitality as a New Frame of Reference

*"...the cry of unfairness ... is, at base,*
*a cry to preserve the order and to uphold the standards..."*
– Norman J. Finkel

*"...L'hospitalité est un rapport social asymétrique..."*
– Anne Gotman

## Introduction

The idea that Canadians have been hoodwinked by their governments (with the complicity of uncritical intelligentsia and media) into accepting a massive and indiscriminate immigration policy as a result of much disinformation and aggressive propaganda for diversity and multiculturalism, is not wrong, but it needs to be contextualized with an appreciation of the compost generated in the 1980s that prepared the ground for this epistemological coup.

One of the most insightful analyses of the transformation of Canada in the post-Charter decade was penned by Richard Gwyn, who had the benefit of being out of the country from the mid-1980s to the early 1990s, and therefore discovered "the unbearable lightness of being Canadian" in the new

Canada when he returned.[80] This transformation provides some keys to an understanding of the bizarre decade, 1995-2005, that followed.

The full force of the multicultural ideology (as strengthened by Article 27 of the Charter committing Canada to preserve and enhance the multicultural heritage of Canadians), and the political *insouciance* when confronted with the Singh decision by the Supreme Court – where the Canadian government did not dare to use the notwithstanding clause when the Supreme Court of Canada (by a three-to-three decision, i.e., one in which the Chief Justice had to cast the deciding vote) ruled in 1985 that a foreigner putting one foot on Canadian soil (legally or not) acquired thereby all the rights and privileges of Canadian citizens, as per Article 7 of the Charter, except the right to vote – can only be ascribed to the Canadian *ethos* having evolved rapidly and dramatically in real time.

The post-Charter decade gave rise to a frenzy of rights; during that period, a Charter that had been put in place to protect the citizen from the state was transformed by identity groups into an instrument to create entitlements of all sorts. During the same period, the Supreme Court also indulged in an irresponsible frenzy of law-making. It was not satisfied to interpret the law; it used the Charter to rewrite the law.

Through a series of decisions, reviewed by Gwyn, (1) the Supreme Court ensured that Article 15(2) of the Charter (about group rights) came to take precedence over Article 15(1) that guaranteed individual rights; and (2) it dramatically extended the ambit of what might legitimately be regarded as a basis for Charter appeal by 'disadvantaged groups,' through an extraordinary broadening of the definition of "disadvantaged group", and a significant extension of the grounds for complaint to include anything that might connote 'chilly climate' or 'hostile environment' – whatever these words might mean.

---

[80] Richard Gwyn. 1995. *Nationalism without Walls – The Unbearable Lightness of Being Canadian*. Toronto: McClelland & Stewart. In particular, part III of this book is a remarkable vignette of the period.

Moreover, the courts in general came to accept as legitimate in their proceedings the notion of 'cultural defence,' based on self-proclaimed beliefs: in a world where most of the population might be able to claim being part of a 'disadvantaged group,' as it is loosely defined, cultural defence based on self-proclaimed cultural beliefs takes the law into a quagmire.[81]

This background explains why it was so easy in the new post-Charter era for a culture of entitlements to flourish, for identity politics to thrive, and for diversity to be politicized. In this context, it became politically incorrect to criticize the new massive and indiscriminate immigration. Indeed, such a regime was promoted as legitimate, acceptable and even honourable.

That new ethos helps to explain the reversal of Canadian views about immigration (as captured in the polls) during the 1995-2005 period – from the mid-1970s to the mid-1990s, when two thirds of the population felt generally that there might be too much immigration, to some 60 percent disagreeing with this proposition by 2005. Such a phenomenal reversal of perspectives (despite the fact that this was a period in which the difficulties of integration were increasing and becoming common knowledge) deserves more attention than it has received.

It most certainly revealed a high degree of false consciousness, a significant gap between the underlying socio-economic realities and the representations concatenated by the diversity/multiculturalism ideology that had been permeating the public consciousness over the preceding decade or so. Indeed, the new ideology had become the new 'Canada brand,' and appeared to be able to filter out any inconvenient truth.

It was not until the second half of the first decade of the 21st century that expressions of concern began to perk up again, as the newcomers' increasing difficulties of integration, and the problems of reasonable and unreasonable accommodation

---

[81] A Canadian county court female judge (Raymonde Verreault) could, in all seriousness, impose on January 13, 1994 a reduced sentence to a man who had assaulted his 11-year old stepdaughter over a two-year period because he had only sodomized her, thereby (in the words of the judge), "preserving her virginity which seems to be a very important value in their (Islamic) religion" (Richard Gwyn, 1995, Part III, p. 197).

demanded by the newcomers, began to reveal a growing apprehension about the impact of the large inflow of immigrants, not only on the socio-economy, but also on the common public culture. However, even over the last few years, these concerns have been expressed only *sotto voce* and anonymously in polls, because they remained unwelcome in public fora. Serious cost studies are still savaged as nativist propaganda, and concerns about the impact on the common public culture of excessively large cohorts of newcomers are completely occluded.

All through those years, critical evaluations of the new immigration policy were met with scorn by the intelligentsia, the officials and the media, while the messages of the choir of immigration lawyers and multiculturalism lobbyists about such critical evaluations being racist and nativist were widely publicized.

This was usually supplemented in the media by an 'alternative explanation' of the new immigrants' increasing difficulties in smoothly integrating into the Canadian socio-economy. It was supposedly entirely due to Canada being a "systemically racist" society – according to a proclamation by Stephen Lewis in his 1992 Report on Racism to the Premier of Ontario.

As amazing as it may be, "this unsubstantiated proclamation was widely accepted as a statement of self-evident truth."[82] Given the historical record of Canada in matters of immigration and integration, one can only regard such a proclamation as not only *ubuesque* but also as a good illustration of the betrayal of intellectuals, and the *holus bolus* acceptance of this proclamation, as evidence of the immense impact of *le pouvoir social*.

If this analysis has any merit, it means that the development of an alternative governance of immigration policy in Canada, and of a more reasonable immigration regime, can only be effected in two steps: first, by challenging the current frame of reference that constitutes a genuine mental prison and prevents effective social learning, and replacing it with an

---

[82] Richard Gwyn, 1995, p. 148-149.

alternative frame of reference that is sounder, more legitimate, and heuristically more powerful – a task tackled in this chapter; and second, by providing, on the basis of this new frame of reference, the sort of array of principles of governance that are to drive the evolving design of a more reasonable immigration regime – a task tackled in chapter 4.

## Moral revolution → social transformation

Changing the frame of reference entails changing the language of problem definition by allowing basic principles to evolve in order to allow a better fit between problems and representations and, thereby, to ease the required social transformation while preserving the integrity (and the reputation) of the organization.[83]

Because the frame of reference evolves through time as the result of experience, it is influenced by the organization's history. But at any one time, it is a nexus of widely shared basic principles that say how things are meant to be done in order for the organization to achieve relatively high levels of effective coordination. This kernel of principles often coalesces around a focal point that defines what is honourable or dishonourable, and influences not only the *tonus* of the common public culture, but the nature of the social arrangements built on it.

The foundational norms and the social arrangements work in tandem: without moral evolution, the needed social arrangements often cannot be designed and take hold. Indeed, Anthony Appiah has argued that a change in the code of honour often allows a necessary social transformation to proceed.[84]

The inter-dynamics between the moral order and the social order do not necessarily always proceed mechanically according to the same sequence: as the context changes, available choice behaviour changes also, and, given appropriate time lags, new

[83] David M. Kreps. 1990. "Corporate Culture and Economic Theory" in James E. Alt and Kenneth A. Shepsle (eds.). *Perspectives on Positive Political Economy.* Cambridge, UK: Cambridge University Press, p. 90-143.

[84] K. Anthony Appiah. 2010. *The Honor Code – How Moral Revolutions Happen.* New York: W.W. Norton.

choice behaviour becomes habitualized into a changed set of principles, and former choice behaviour becomes less and less appropriate, and therefore unacceptable.[85]

## Frame of reference I

In the modern Canada of the late 20th century, where nobody is fully in charge, and where there are no common values,[86] individuals have developed a strong sense of entitlements. The philosophy of human rights has come to dominate the scene. Moreover, those entitlements or rights, when not honoured, led to claims of victimization, humiliation, dishonourable treatment, etc., all the more so when such entitlement was perceived as entrenched in the Charter. Frame of reference I prevails.

It all began in the 1940s with the Universal Declaration of Human Rights and the inclination of the 'welfare state' to put the declaration at the centre of its agenda. But this movement accelerated in Canada after the 1982 Charter was put in place.

Even though the Charter was meant to protect the citizen from the state, it has been twisted somewhat into an instrument to manufacture entitlements. As the Canadian identity was becoming unbearably light (and maybe because of that), it has come to be defined by entitlements like Medicare. Groups have followed suit and charters of rights of prisoners, or patients, or the like have popped up. There has also been a tendency for these entitlements to be judiciarized, and to become ossified or ratcheted up over time. This has become the ruling philosophy in Canada.

This has been fully exploited by the multiculturalism ideologues and theorized by Berry, Taylor and Kymlicka. Their claim was that newcomers could not fully develop as individuals, and therefore could not integrate well in the new society, without appropriate recognition of their specificity and without the active preservation of a supportive homeland-

---

[85] Immanuel G. Mesthene. 1970. *Technological Change: Its Impact on Man and Society.* New York: Mentor.

[86] Gilles Paquet. 1999. "Innovations in Governance in Canada," *Optimum,* 29(2/3): 71-81; Joseph Heath. 2003. *The Myth of Shared Values in Canada.* Ottawa: Canadian Centre for Management Development.

related cultural milieu in the host society. Consequently, it was determined that they were 'entitled' to such support and recognition. This underlying argument underpins the frame of reference in good currency during the 1990s, and it has been summarized in an earlier book.[87]

Three contextual features may be said to have been catalyzed and re-enforced by the impact of the Charter: the fundamentalism of entitlements, the idolatry of the rights language, and the despotism of political correctness.

## The fundamentalism of entitlements

The complex dynamics of the citizen's claims in the name of real or imaginary entitlements (and of state-centricity as a mechanism to ensure that these entitlements will be honoured) had already created a vicious self-reinforcing cycle in the world of the 'welfare state.' Post-war governments have thrived at the electoral level by inventing a large number of entitlements without paying any attention to the sort of wealth generation necessary to finance them, or to the sort of **de-responsibilization** of the citizen that might be triggered by such paternalism.

Welfare-state governments not only graciously bestowed free public goods and services on the citizens, but they also persuaded the citizens that they were 'entitled' to these goods and services. Canadians developed an 'entitlement speak,' and their sense of responsibility for their own sustenance and survival went to sleep. The Charter, echoing the enthusiasm of its time, dramatically bolstered this sense of entitlement and conveyed to Canadians that it would not only ensure freedom from state intrusion, but also, and most importantly, that it would underwrite or guarantee these entitlements to state benefits.

This indoctrination was so successful that the very definition of Canadian citizenship came to be reduced to a bouquet of such entitlements in many public debates: Canadian identity becoming confused with Medicare benefits and the

---

[87] Gilles Paquet. 2008. *Deep Cultural Diversity – A Governance Challenge*. Ottawa: University of Ottawa Press, p. 138ff. The following paragraphs borrow freely from this section of the book.

like. Interpreted in an egalitarianistic frame of mind by the courts, the Charter became an invitation for all groups feeling relatively disadvantaged, or having preferences different from the majority, to ask for remedial action, and to argue that equality in the Charter was not to be interpreted as equality of opportunity, but equality of outcome.

This inflation of entitlements was considerably bolstered by the crippling epistemology[88] that has permeated the whole socio-political system as a result of the impact of the Berry-Taylor doctrine that came to be in good currency in the first decade after the Charter.

This doctrine stemmed from the same delusional world that brought forth egalitarianism – sentimentality, indiscriminate compassion, and a deep narcissism of the tribe from which supposedly one should not be weaned.[89] It developed an approach to deep diversity in a plural society based on two basic propositions: (1) **the multicultural assumption** that asserts that only those who are secure in their ethno-cultural background will be open to others, tolerant toward others, and capable of integrating within the host society (John Berry) and (2) **the politics of recognition** that asserts that such an integration-prone setting can best be achieved through an explicit recognition of the ethno-cultural identity *per se* of these persons and groups, and of all that such a recognition entails (Charles Taylor).[90]

These two propositions clearly reinforce each other, and produce a psycho-social dynamic that provides much support for multiculturalism as a strategy. Both have been accepted,

---

[88] Russell Hardin. 2002. "The Crippled Epistemology of Extremism" in Albert Breton et al. (eds.). *Political Extremisms and Rationality*. Cambridge, UK: Cambridge University Press, p. 3-22.

[89] John Kekes. 2003. *The Illusions of Egalitarianism*. Ithaca, NY: Cornell University Press, chapter 13.

[90] Although there have been many versions of these two 'propositions' the canonical ones are J.W. Berry, R. Kalin and D. Taylor. 1977. *Multiculturalism and Ethnic Attitudes in Canada*. Ottawa: Supply and Services Canada; and Charles Taylor. 1992. *Multiculturalism and the Politics of Recognition*. Princeton: Princeton University Press.

without much critical thinking, as providing the theoretical foundation for the Canadian strategy. This canonical version has been extended by Will Kymlicka, who has added the feature of affirmative action being required to repair not only present but past cultural prejudices.[91]

Yet these propositions are contestable.

They tend to allow certain cultural features to be dominant and almost exclusive markers for persons or groups, and to suggest that formal and official recognition (and therefore their reification in their present state) of these markers as foundational should be pursued to the exclusion of, or at least in preference to others, by active support of the state.

This shaky theorization provided an intellectual scaffold to support a particular strategy of integration built on (1) a hardening of cultural differences and (2) a crucial importance being given to the redistribution of resources (for recognition entails redistribution), based on the egalitarian philosophy that all cultures are equal and have the same rights.

The fundamentalism of cultural entitlements generated by egalitarianism and the Charter has become immunized from critical evaluation by both the aura of legitimacy bestowed on these entitlements because they are couched in a language of rights, and by the added protection of political correctness that allows spurious beliefs and groundless presumptions to escape challenge.

So the Berry-Taylor *problématique* has become the new canon, and has received both academic and political accolades.[92]

### The seduction of the rights language

One of the major defence mechanisms against critical thinking is the wholesale adoption of the language of rights. This is a potent rhetorical device. Rights have an aura of legitimacy as

---

[91] Will Kymlicka. 1995. *Multicultural Citizenship*. Oxford, UK: Oxford University Press.

[92] Gilles Paquet. 1994. "Political Philosophy of Multiculturalism" in John Berry et al. (eds.). *Ethnicity and Culture in Canada*. Toronto: University of Toronto Press, p. 60-80; also Gilles Paquet, 2008.

if they were the result of 'virgin birth' based on high principles and, therefore, not obvious candidates for any debate. Few remember that they are the result of political haggling and discussion in legislatures that one could not always describe as enlightened.

This sort of nimbus may be said to have emerged in the 1940s when the Universal Declaration of Human Rights (covering a whole range of economic, social and political *desiderata*) was put forward as an ideal to be pursued. This did much to blur into an amalgam notions like rights, preferences, ideals and the like. In the welfare-state era, more and more precedence was given to security over freedom and autonomy, and this document became a blueprint of entitlements to be acquired.

The rhetorical power of such claims led to a displacement of the language of needs (always contestable) by the language of rights (that claimed not to be contestable). Michael Ignatieff labels this discontinuity as a move from "rights as politics" to "rights as idolatry".[93]

The central idea is that human rights have drifted from connoting pragmatic political instruments designed to protect human agency against abuse, oppression and degradation (something identified with negative liberty), to connoting any aspiration or anything desirable being pronounced a right on the basis that some felt it necessary (with or without any foundation to that claim) for the individual to develop as fully as he/she can or would like (something identified with positive liberty).

As Michael Ignatieff points out, since legitimate core rights are a "tool kit against oppression", one should not automatically define anything desirable as a right, because that is bound to erode the legitimacy of core rights. In Canada, so-called disadvantaged groups have come to define all sorts of things as a right guaranteed by the Charter – from being allowed to bring one's homosexual boyfriend to the high school prom, to receiving welfare benefits even though one lives with a spouse

---

[93] Michael Ignatieff. 2001. *Human Rights as Politics and Idolatry*. Princeton: Princeton University Press.

who can financially afford to support the entire household. This has led to an abuse of the rights language.

## A despotism of political correctness

The dynamics triggered by the dominance of the concept of right evoked above (especially when robustly propelled by judicial activism)[94] has entailed not only an inflation of rights, but a dominance of **righteousness**. This sleight of hand has allowed the courts to entertain any complaint about wishes in the clothing of rights. In normal times in a normal country, such excesses would have been contained by strong voices from civil society or from vigilant legislatures. But this is not the case in countries where deference and political correctness have become major forces in certain domains, and where 'progressivism' (often defined as the ideological lever used whenever what one wants to propose as policy one cannot persuasively defend on rational grounds) is the new North Star.

Political correctness has prevented the denunciation of 'luxury rights' for fear of being branded non-progressive; this has led to an orgy of frivolous cases. Indeed, claiming anything as a right has become a standard conversation and deliberation stopper.

This new despotism of political correctness has left elected officials so intimidated by the Charter and its rhetoric that they have routinely chosen not to challenge the courts, even when the rulings were clearly unreasonable (as in the Singh case where the court decision entailed a loss of control on the country's borders). This is the case even though the elected officials had the necessary tools to restrain the courts – the notwithstanding clause. But the false aura of the Charter has been such that governments have proved incapable of articulating anything but timid and unpersuasive responses to undesirable court decisions, and have even failed to convince the rights-minded population that invoking the notwithstanding clause would not necessarily curtail their freedom.

[94] Rory Leishman. 2006. *Against Judicial Activism – The decline of freedom and democracy in Canada*. Montreal and Kingston: McGill-Queen's University Press.

## Common public culture under threat

The Berry-Taylor argument may sound rather innocuous when a host society is faced with minuscule immigrant communities that may take some time in integrating and need some help in doing so at their own pace. However, when, as in the case of Canada, already almost one person out of four has been born outside the country – and it is anticipated, if the present immigration policy continues, that the ratio may be closer to one out of three some 30 years from now – the immigration policy and the multiculturalist philosophy are like the two blades of a pair of scissors that are bound to fundamentally transform the common public culture, the way in which Canadians, over centuries, have chosen to organize their *vivre-ensemble*.

The Canadian common public culture is a nebula. It is a compounding of the basic principles and essential beliefs that underpin the conventions and moral contracts that organize our *vivre-ensemble*. These principles and beliefs have developed over time, and represent the outcome of an evolutionary process blending both some genetic-cultural co-evolutionary factors inherited from our humanity, and some more idiosyncratic features attached to our own organizational culture.[95]

What made the Canadian case special is that Canadians were not only swayed by the gospel of moral relativism like many other societies, but have come to be further swayed, so to speak, by the ideological propaganda referred to in the last section: sufficiently to come to believe that not only is there no ordering of values, but no ordering of cultures, either. Officials would even state that Canada had no Canadian identity, "no national culture"[96] and that therefore newcomers could bring their own culture with them when migrating

---

[95] Samuel Bowles and Herbert Gintis. 2011. *A Cooperative Species – Human Reciprocity and its Evolution*. Princeton: Princeton University Press; Gilles Paquet. 2011. *Gouvernance collaborative: un anti manuel*. Montreal: Liber, chapters 3-4.

[96] Richard Gwyn, 1995, p. 182.

to Canada. As a result, Canadians have been led to sleepwalk unwittingly into an erosion of their own evolving common public culture. The intelligentsia, the political officials and the media led the parade and staunchly defended this equality of all cultures as acceptable and desirable: none can be declared better or worse than any other. This led naturally to the host society being driven to accommodate to the cultures of newcomers.

Even asking if there might not be limits to such accommodation, and maybe elements of the host society's common public culture that can legitimately be declared to be non-negotiable, has proved to be a controversial proposition. Yet the whole common public culture[97] very much depends on some set of main common principles, and may legitimately differ from one part of the world to another and be deemed worthy of preservation.[98]

Some of the features of our common public culture may be more or less desirable from a moral or a survival point of view for the community. For instance, concern about the survival of the French language in Quebec has led some opinion moulders to suggest that the indiscriminate flow of new immigrants in Quebec should be contained until such time as more effective selection mechanisms, more explicit terms of engagement and integration, and better supportive integration structures are in place to ensure that the newcomers are most likely to become part of the French-speaking community. There is a fear that the 'Frenchness' of the whole community might unwittingly be significantly eroded by massive indiscriminate immigration.

Given the present frame of reference based on entitlements and rights, and the Berry-Taylor doctrine in good currency, one is faced with conflicting imperatives (the entitlements of the newcomers versus the entitlements of the

[97] Gary Caldwell. 2001. *La culture publique commune.* Quebec: Éditions Nota Bene.
[98] Michèle Lamont and Laurent Thévenot (eds.). 2000. *Rethinking Comparative Cultural Sociology, Repertoires of Evaluation in France and in the United States.* Cambridge, UK: Cambridge University Press.

*citoyens de souche*), and the **frame of reference I** (the one in good currency in the last decades) offers very little in the way of determining what might be regarded as 'reasonable accommodation' between imperatives that are presented as quasi-absolutes.

What is required is a frame of reference that is more legitimate than the sheer conflict of absolute entitlements and more heuristically powerful in guiding the process of reasonable accommodation between older and newer Canadians. This transition to a new frame of reference entails nothing less than a moral revolution that would change the nature of what is or is not regarded as honourable.

## Frame of reference II in the making

As we mentioned earlier, the old moral code, anchored in egalitarianism, status, identity and entitlements, has led to the common public culture giving signs of erosion with massive and indiscriminate immigration, both because the terms of integration have remained opaque and thin, and because newcomers have quite naturally taken advantage of the prevalent entitlement-inspired frame of reference to demand ever more significant accommodation. As the relative importance of the foreign-born population grew, they were able to demand further accommodation, and it can only be anticipated that, as their demographic weight increases yet further, their beliefs will come to prevail and to transform what we have meant by *homo Canadensis*.[99]

Identity politics, its apparatus of entitlements, and its trolley of claims of victimization and humiliation, remains obviously a *force majeure* in Canada. The media reports daily on new Charter-type initiatives of supposedly disadvantaged groups and on the victimization of such groups when their wishes are not met. Indignation provides legitimacy.

[99] Richard Gwyn, 1995, chapter 13.

But in a world of surfusion[100] like ours, some minor events often trigger important changes. And it may be said that the commotion created in Quebec by the local officials of Hérouxville (who decided to draft some dos-and-don'ts in the form of a local code of behaviour, defining some sort of moral contract with newcomers) was such a shock that the Quebec government decided to create a special commission (chaired by Gérard Bouchard and Charles Taylor) to study what might be regarded as reasonable and unreasonable accommodation between newcomers and *citoyens de souche*.[101]

The final report was predictably in line with the conventional frame of reference, and concluded that the Quebec population should bear the brunt of the accommodation. This was also, predictably, rejected by the citizenry.

Consequently, the report of the commission was unceremoniously shelved. But the process of discussion initiated by the commission was quite important in beginning to transform the frame of reference for the discussion of immigration. In Quebec, the topic ceased to be a taboo topic. Less so, more slowly and painfully but significantly, in the rest of Canada it marked the beginning of a shift from a debate

---

[100] Surfusion is a physical state that can change dramatically as a result of a very small shock. Hubert Reeves has illustrated this physical phenomenon by referring to a 1942 event when 1,000 horses threatened by a forest fire jumped in Lake Ladoga to save their lives. Even though the temperature had dropped sharply in the last previous days, the lake was still liquid. But as the horses swam to the other side of the lake, the whole lake suddenly froze. The day after, the horses were found transformed into ice monuments at the centre of the lake. Reeves explained that when the drop in temperature is too rapid, the water does not have time to freeze and remains liquid at temperatures below zero. But water is unstable, and the lightest shock may trigger a process of instant crystallization (Hubert Reeves. 1986. *L'art de s'enivrer*. Paris: Le Seuil). This phenomenon also applies to organizations (Gilles Paquet. 2011. "Le nationalisme québécois dans une ère de surfusion" in Gilles Paquet, *Tableau d'avancement II – Essais exploratoires sur la gouvernance d'un certain Canada français*. Ottawa: Invenire, chapter 10).

[101] La Commission de consultation sur les pratiques d'accommodement reliées aux différences culturelles was created in 2007 and the final report (*Fonder l'avenir – Le temps de la conciliation*) was tabled in 2008.

about identity, status and rights, toward a new discussion that was focused on relationships, negotiations, and terms of integration.

This new focus of conversation has not completely eclipsed the old debate about identity and status, but it has triggered a slow process of **refocusing** on the need for some basis on which to construct the sort of negotiation and conciliation that would appear to be necessary to arbitrate between newcomers and *citoyens de source*, but also among the different groups in a pluralist society. The question that all had carefully avoided as not discussable until then – what one might legitimately regard as negotiable and non-negotiable in the common public culture – has now become recognized as one that has to be discussed.

There has been a craving for core principles that one might be able to build on in such negotiations. The challenge is to come up with something more legitimate than the conventional zero-sum-game battle of entitlements in this sort of conversation.

In my view, the Bouchard-Taylor chautauqua (not its documents) has revealed a certain sense of the *essoufflement* of identity politics, a need to focus rather on the centrality of relationships,[102] and the possibility of building on the elusive notions of **fair play** and **hospitality** as the basis for a useful democratic conversation about immigration in a pluralist society.

These two notions are in creative tension: fair play connotes symmetry and reciprocity, while hospitality connotes asymmetry and conditionality. They posit the dual terms on which the immigration regime hinges, and on which the moral contracts between newcomers and *citoyens de souche* are constructed: the need to ensure fair play in the process and in the outcome of the admission and integration of newcomers in the host society, while recognizing that admission and integration into a new society must be conducted under the asymmetric conditions of hospitality imposed by the host society as long as they are reasonable.

[102] Paul Laurent and Gilles Paquet. 1998. *Epistémologie et économie de la relation.* Paris/Lyon: Vrin.

This fair-play-with-conditional-hospitality framework provides a foundation for the definition and redefinition over time of the moral contracts between newcomers and old citizens. Indeed, the moral contracts embody the balancing act between the symmetry of fair play and the asymmetry of hospitality.

### Fair play as standard

Even though the notion of **fair play** has not been mentioned explicitly in the current debates on immigration, it has been there in all but explicit name and, for obvious reasons, because it may be regarded as a sort of golden rule ("I do unto you what I would have you do unto me") that would appear to be acceptable across cultures and even across species. It has even been suggested that we are wired to behave in this way toward others.[103]

Whether one agrees on fair play as a golden rule, or as something of more limited value,[104] the notion of fair play establishes a **standard** that is widely regarded as having to be respected in all matters of collaboration and negotiation. In the case of the integration of immigrants, the sense of reasonableness implied by that principle excludes both forms of extremism – the denial of any accommodation to make life bearable for the newcomers and the complete subordination of the foundational principles of the host population to the whims of newcomers.

Human reciprocity and human cooperation are key features of our species. Indeed, the prevailing explanation for the emergence of this cooperative species is based on some sort of gene-culture co-evolution.[105] In the process of conciliation between newcomers and *citoyens de souche*, one may then count on fair play being a rough rule of thumb of reciprocity that has some foundation in the evolution of our species, and is likely to be much more legitimate than the brandishing of entitlements based on questionable political haggling.

---

[103] Donald W. Pfaff. 2007. *The Neuroscience of Fair Play*. New York: Dana Press.

[104] Patricia S. Churchland. 2011. *Braintrust – What neuroscience tells us about morality*. Princeton: Princeton University Press.

[105] Samuel Bowles and Herbert Gintis. 2011. *A Cooperative Species – Human Reciprocity and its Evolution*. Princeton: Princeton University Press.

## *Fair play does not mean symmetry in all dimensions*

In the case of immigration and diversity in a pluralist society, the values and preferences of the different groups are bound to diverge. What fair play would mean as a kernel principle is that, in the process of defining reasonable accommodations, it would become a guidepost both on substance and form. It would protect individuals on two fronts: first, it would ensure that individuals cannot be forced to organize their whole life around their race, their language, their sexuality, their religion or other such markers, for such an enforcement of identity would be a form of social tyranny. Second, fair play would protect individuals from the tyranny of any manufactured common values and only seek to get agreement on certain principles and standards that the diverse parties would agree to commit to (often for very different reasons) in order to ensure a civilized and decent society. A civilized and decent society is one in which its members do not humiliate one another, and where its institutions do not humiliate anyone, either.[106]

Negotiations and conciliation would be conducted in a manner that would generate an outcome not bowing to the preferences and idiosyncrasies of any group. They would ensure that the needs for a decent and civilized society are maintained. A host society is not simply a bingo hall that one can join fleetingly, but a society that has historically established rules of *vivre-ensemble* that need to be fully acknowledged as a basic minimal common public culture that the newcomers need to take into account in their terms of integration.

The fact that newcomers cannot join a host society as members without paying attention to the prevailing rules of their new home's *vivre-ensemble* entails a certain asymmetry in the accommodation process. Because one, for example, used to drive on the left side of the street in the home country, one cannot expect to be able to do it in the host country where driving on the right side of the street has been in good currency for ages.

[106] Avishai Margalit. 1996. *The Decent Society*. Cambridge, MA: Harvard University Press.

The key challenge would be to determine what can and cannot be negotiated, and to do so with fair play in mind, but in full cognition and recognition that certain rules of *vivre-ensemble* in the common public culture of the host society will not be negotiable.

## Fair play and moral contracts

The expression *"la paix des braves"* has come to be used as a way to capture the results of negotiations that leave all parties with a sense of having agreed on an honourable settlement. Such settlements do not necessarily leave all parties equally happy, or treat them necessarily in a completely even or similar way, but they are regarded as acceptable, and as having saved face for all.

History has shown that any peace settlement that does not meet this criterion ends up fuelling much resentment in certain quarters, and generating further conflicts later, often of an even more serious sort. This is why the sort of moral contracts in which these arrangements are embodied must be carefully crafted with a full appreciation of the whole psycho-social context.

Over 20 years ago, Mme Gagnon-Tremblay and colleagues[107] tabled a white paper suggesting that Quebec should negotiate moral contracts with newcomers. Such an approach was considered unacceptable by officials in Ottawa at the time and denounced in vicious terms. Yet it probably represented the first creative effort to deal with the swamping effects of the new immigration regime in a manner that would build on a less constricted frame of reference.[108] This was done in a spirit that is not unlike what was proposed much later by Anthony Appiah – a recognition that identities matter, but that neutrality does not mean that "anything goes": the host society accommodates difference where it can, but is not bound to preserve particular cultures.[109]

---

[107] Monique Gagnon-Tremblay et al. 1990. *Au Québec, pour bâtir ensemble.* Quebec: Governement de Québec.

[108] Gilles Paquet. December 15, 1990. "De l'État protecteur au contrat moral," *Le Devoir.*

[109] K. Anthony Appiah. 2004. *The Ethics of Identity.* Princeton: Princeton University Press.

This initiative was obviously premature in 1990. It was regarded as incompatible with the gospel of multiculturalism, even though it was not trying to formulate formal legally-binding agreements but only to negotiate informal moral contracts that would clarify mutual expectations and that would recognize the fluid, multiple identities of newcomers. It was unacceptable in Ottawa because it was seen as explicitly countering what multiculturalism was propounding, i.e., reifying the culture – an argument that Appiah would pick up later in his criticism of multiculturalism.

The principle of fair play would help define such contracts in an even handed way, while recognizing the need for the practices to conform to liberal standards, for instance, in a country like Canada. What the tenor of the moral contracts should be, and the ways in which they should be allowed to evolve, are not my concern here – we shall return to this question in chapter 4 – but it is clear, in my own mind, that they should have a **liberal cosmopolitanism flavour.**

Cosmopolitans value diversity for what it makes possible for human agency and recognize the value-adding that comes with accommodation, but acknowledge that there are elements of the host society's common public culture that command respect. Consequently, what Appiah calls "rooted cosmopolitanism" commands respect for common humanity, shared understanding of narratives, but also local attachments and experience, for these are necessary to provide existential stability through the intergenerational continuity of important symbols.

This new frame of reference, based on fair play, would have to build on an explicit understanding of what is meant by absorptive capacity: the relationships between the host society and the newcomers; and, the capacity to integrate newcomers effectively in a manner that is technically feasible, socially acceptable, implementable, and not too politically destabilizing. There may be differences of opinion about what this might mean, but one should be able to identify broad guideposts scoping the boundaries of what would be generally regarded as a workable corridor.

## Hospitality and asymmetry

The **frame of reference I**, with its focus on entitlements and equality of cultures, has evolved the view that any newcomer has the right to choose to belong to any community he chooses to join, on his own terms, in the name of a common human condition.[110] This is clearly abusive. Any newcomer has a right to apply for membership in a new community, but hospitality is an asymmetric social relationship: not having contributed to the construction of the host society`s social capital, the newcomer has to receive permission to join, either on the basis of a demonstration that he can contribute to the host society in the future, or as the result of permission granted as a sheer act of unrequited kindness. It cannot be assumed that any newcomer has an absolute right to become a member in the host society only because this newcomer wants to. The newcomer must meet the conditions for membership decreed by the host community.

The **frame of reference II** builds on fairness in defining the laws of hospitality and in negotiating the moral contracts defining the terms of admission, engagement and integration into the host society. This entails a fair process and different *mises à l'épreuve* (ways of putting newcomers to the test) that may be defined differentially by different host communities, depending on what they wish to preserve or re-enforce in their communities, and what they regard as of secondary importance, and therefore contingent. These rules need not give access by newcomers to a single status; there may be differential degrees of access, and various levels of membership, and the status granted may be subject to repeal under certain conditions.

Defining an immigration regime is defining *les lois de l'hospitalité* of the host society – the more or less well-defined conditions of admissibility, ways of insertion and engagement in the host society and the help to be provided in so doing, terms of integration, and the process through which the newcomer

---

[110] Pierre Centlivres. 1997. "Hospitalité, État et naturalisation : l'exemple suisse," *Communications*, (65): 99-107.

will gain access to the range of rights and responsibilities of the full-fledged citizen.[111]

This approach to immigration underlines the asymmetry of the relationship between the newcomer and the host society, legitimizes the apparatus of conditions and *épreuves* (tests) that must be satisfied for the newcomer to be admitted and promoted to the rank of citizen, and entails a burden of office for the citizen – a battery of expectations about the behaviour, the duties and responsibilities, and the rights and privileges attached to citizenship.

The displacement of the former frame of reference – the one based on entitlements and rights – by the latter – based on fair play in relationships and hospitality – is proceeding very slowly and painfully in Canada.

The notion of citizenship has remained prevalently anchored in a legal status very much in line with the former framework of reference. Traditionally, citizenship has inhered in individuals who are seen as bearers of rights and it was couched in a language of entitlements. Individuals were required to do very little in order to become and remain Canadian citizens.

The **framework of reference II** sees citizenship much differently. Citizens are producers of governance, and the definition of citizenship is couched in terms of duties and participation. Newcomers are chosen and *mis à l'épreuve* to see if they are qualified to become members of the community, to participate in the culture and governance of the community. This gives a great deal of importance to belonging.

The unbearable lightness of being a Canadian in the former frame of reference is indeed what has made the massive and indiscriminate immigration regime so easy to accept: bringing newcomers in was seen as quite inconsequential, like adding a few tables in a bingo hall, where conditions of admission are trivial. This very 'thin' notion of citizenship is quite unacceptable in the latter frame of reference: citizenship becomes a much 'thicker' notion there, something that is

---

[111] Daniel Innerarity. 2009. *Éthique de l'hospitalité*. Quebec: Presses de l'Université Laval.

consequential because of its impact on the Canadian economy, polity and society, and on the common public culture and governance of the country. The new framework entails more rigorous selection criteria, and much more rigorous definitions of terms of integration for newcomers.

It is well recognized that few countries have been as lax as Canada in governing her immigration regime, as loose in defining the conditions of admission and the terms of integration, and as insouciant in maintaining control of her borders. Indeed, this is the reason why Canada is faced with the challenges described above. Moreover, multiculturalism as a philosophy (whatever its generous intentions) has made it extremely difficult to define strict *lois de l'hospitalité*, because what has been in good currency in Switzerland or in Australia has come to be regarded in Canada (through the lens of multiculturalism) as unacceptably restrictive and not sufficiently generous – another word for indiscriminate and irresponsible compassion.

What has emerged in the last few years is a new awareness that the present language of problem definition is quite unsuitable to deal with the challenges created in our pluralistic society, and that we need new mechanisms of solidarity that will demand more from citizens (old and new) if these challenges are to be met.

So while these pressures go counter the moral relativism of the day, they are beginning to be felt sufficiently strongly that they cannot be ignored. Consequently, the fair play in designing a hospitality regime that will select better and more wisely those who can contribute positively to Canada's future, is not as un-discussable as it might have been 20 years ago. How far can moral contracts with newcomers go in defining *les nouvelles lois de l'hospitalité* may not be clear to all at this time, but what has become clear is that the costs of inaction on this front have become important enough, and loom so large for the future, that it is no longer possible to put off our best effort now. Some cautious experiments and propositions are now being considered and tried out: this may show that the timing for something more ambitious is right.

## Conclusion

The shift from a focus on rights and entitlements to a focus on relationships, fair play, and hospitality cannot easily be completed without a change in the code of honour – in the notion of what is honourable. In the old framework, entitlements are absolutes, and compromises are a source of dishonour and of loss of face. In the new framework, imaginative compromises are superior honourable solutions.

That is why the model for the new framework of reference is *"la paix des braves"*, and what has to be sought in arriving at a fair play compromise on the immigration issue is to ensure that all parties find that the negotiated accommodation is regarded as preserving the essential on all sides.

This cannot be achieved unless the immigration policy as an inquiring system is capable of learning what all parties regard as fair, of translating those beliefs into arrangements that are mutually compatible, and of meeting the standards that the host society regards as falling within the realm of absorptive capacity – i.e., meeting the four basic constraints (being technically feasible, socially acceptable, implementable and not too politically destabilizing). The inquiring system must also be capable of adjusting as smoothly as possible in the face of evolving internal and external environments, while not unduly straining the common public culture by requiring unduly abrupt adjustments.

The code of honour and the hospitality arrangements that meet the principle of fair play are the tip of the ethical iceberg: what is regarded as honourable and fair must in normal times be ethical in the triple sense of stemming from good motives (ethics of character), following good rules (ethics of duty), and leading to good outcomes (ethics of utility). Consequently the search for a principled immigration regime will require being able to demonstrate that it meets these different criteria.

The next chapter sketches the principles that might serve as a foundation for such an immigration regime as inquiring systems.

# CHAPTER 4
## | Toward Principled Governance of the Immigration Regime

*"...N'abusez pas du Samaritain..."*
*— Jacques Perret*

## Introduction

To get the job done, it is not sufficient to identify some foundations for the reframing of the immigration regime. One must also build on those new foundations a general philosophy and some meaningful principles, norms, rules and criteria to anchor a principled governance of the immigration regime that would meet the standards of a code of honour, built on hospitality, fairness and reasonable accommodation.

This entails an operational definition of absorptive capacity in terms of hospitality, fairness, the protection of the host society's common public culture, and the design of an inquiring system that will ensure effective social learning as circumstances change.[112]

[112] An immigration regime does not simply connote mechanisms to reach some goals through some control processes, but a process of 'wayfinding,' based on intelligence and innovation, aimed at keeping the organization within a certain corridor of economic, social, and cultural acceptability through experimentation. Gilles Paquet and Christopher Wilson. 2011. "Collaborative Co-governance as Inquiring Systems," *www.optimumonline.ca*, 41(2): 1-12; see also, Ruth Hubbard, Gilles Paquet and Christopher Wilson. 2012. *Stewardship – Collaborative Decentred Metagovernance and Inquiring Systems*. Ottawa: Invenire.

The next sections clarify these issues and outline the basic philosophy of immigration that ensues; provide a circumspect appraisal of the concerns raised and not raised in officialdom about the present immigration arrangements; and, sketch the broad contours of the set of repairs and initiatives that might define a principled governance of the Canadian immigration regime and can be progressively implemented – beginning with the less controversial and culminating with the more difficult to negotiate. In closing, some suggestions are made about the terms of integration that this approach would lead to, and about the default settings that need to be put in place to ensure that the immigration regime has some fail-safe mechanisms in case the inquiring system should lead the host society outside its corridor of acceptability – economic, social and cultural.

## Basic philosophy

### Cosmopolitanism as an alternative reference

To exorcize the bizarre infatuation with multiculturalism, one has to rise to the challenge of providing an alternative cosmology that may be favourably compared with the current one. Anthony Appiah has provided such an alternative cosmology[113] – the **intermediate cosmopolitanism perspective** – that Appiah defines as a meshing of two strands: the ideas of obligations to others, and taking an interest in them and learning from them. The cosmopolitan relates to others in a way that is neither utopian (all human beings and cultures being treated as equals is both unnatural and unrealistic) nor entirely disconnected (strangers being regarded as of another species is also unacceptable except by bigots). Cosmopolitans follow a third way. They presume that even though all cultures are not equal, they "have enough overlap in their vocabulary of values to begin a conversation".[114]

This does not presume that there will be an agreement, but that there will be a conversation. Cosmopolitanism is connection, not through more robust identity affirmation

---

[113] K. Anthony Appiah. 2006. *Cosmopolitanism*. New York: Norton, p. xv.
[114] K. Anthony Appiah, 2006, p. 57.

and recognition, (generating a hardening of the boundaries) but connection despite difference.[115] In that sense, cosmopolitanism is the obverse of multiculturalism, which wishes to establish connection through building stronger separate identity claims and arguing, as the Berry-Taylor doctrine would have it, that more robust recognition of such claims will make connections easier.

Radically strong cosmopolitanism is a fanciful notion: the idea that each of us has equal responsibilities to all persons worldwide is utopian. And radically weak cosmopolitanism (boutique cosmopolitanism), based on the most superficial interest in exoticism and the like, is anodyne. But **intermediate cosmopolitanism** is neither anodyne nor utopian. It asserts that "all persons have a negative duty ... toward every human being not to collaborate in imposing an unjust institutional order upon him or her,"[116] and it adds that special 'thicker' relationships can increase what we feel we owe to closer associates (family, compatriots, etc.), but that they cannot decrease what we owe everyone else.

This intermediate cosmopolitanism is a necessary reference through which one might be able to appraise other strategies to cope with deep cultural diversity. It is a crucial reference since it provides a meaningful counterpoint for the ideology in good currency, and an essential tool to topple the canonical ideology – for only a more intellectually satisfying alternative cosmology can undermine the invisible multicultural elephant in the room by revealing its very contestable foundations.

Becoming cosmopolitan will not be possible without some cultural change and without denouncing many mental prisons. And it will take time. Having a counter-reference should help in revealing the features of the current dominant ideology that make it contestable. Moreover, it is difficult to challenge a cosmology without offering an alternative one in its stead. Consequently, one may hope that

[115] K. Anthony Appiah, 2006, p. 135.

[116] Thomas W. Pogge. 2002. "Cosmopolitanism: A Defence," *Critical Review of International Social and Political Philosophy*, 5(3): 89.

intermediate cosmopolitanism may indeed, with a modicum of explanation, come to replace over time the current ruling ideology of multiculturalism and tend to support a reformed immigration regime.

## Hospitality as a function of absorptive capacity

Hospitality means recognizing the needs of strangers and bestowing on them gratifications of many sorts, among them, the permission to become a member of one's own community. However, such permission is not to be granted lightly and unconditionally, and the process used should not be arbitrary and whimsical. The permission to become a member should be one that will be equally beneficial to both the newcomers and the citizens of the host society. This is the case when the host society's capabilities and functioning are not unduly impaired by the arrival of the newcomers.

When, at times, the conditions of the host society become precarious (economically, socially, culturally, security-wise, etc.), the flow of newcomers to be absorbed should then reasonably be curtailed and more carefully sifted. For very high indiscriminate inflows of newcomers may not only reduce the welfare of members of the host society, but also be detrimental to the newcomers themselves, who might find it most painful to fit into a socio-economy that has great difficulty generating jobs and income for those already there.

Absorptive capacity does not only refer to temporary physical capacity, or even the economic capacity to absorb the newcomers, but also to the capacity for the host society to maintain and preserve whatever characteristics and features are regarded as of importance as a way to ensure the preservation of the common public culture, and the capacity of *vivre ensemble* that has been nurtured and has evolved over time. Hospitality entails conditionality. It does not mean allowing the guests to move in as a matter of right and, wittingly or unwittingly, being allowed to transform the way of life of the host society in an abrupt manner.

In a summary and somewhat vivid way of restating the above, hospitality must avoid falling into the trap portrayed in the parable of the dishonest tenants.

In this parable, a man of goodwill allows his tenants to husband a portion of his vineyard. When at the end of the season he sends a servant to collect from the tenants his portion of the fruit of the vineyards, the tenants beat the servant and send him away empty. After many additional efforts to collect his due, the man sends his son thinking that they would revere his son. The tenants then kill the son in the hope that the inheritance would be theirs. This situation could only degenerate into further violence. Indeed, in the parable, it is said that the owner of the vineyard destroyed the tenants and rented the vineyard to others who would respect their moral contract.

The whole process of conditional admission to membership in the new society must be played out in ways that are free from bias, dishonesty and unfairness, but with due diligence, and taking into account the legitimate concerns of the host society.

In that sense, fair play implies a triple set of standards: legitimate processes, acceptable and effective outcomes, and arrangements that leave partners with a sense that the arrangement is honorable, as in "*la paix des braves*". But fair play does not necessarily have to leave all the parties equally or totally satisfied with the outcomes. If any party defines honour in such a way that it demands unacceptable concessions from the host society (as in the case of honour crimes, or cultural practices that are in flagrant violation of the host society's common public culture), fair play does not command that they be met.

### Moral contract as basic tool

When it comes to successful integration into the host society, what is clear is that it is a process that requires mutual adjustment by both the newcomers and the host society. Up to now, this has been handled in a most insouciant way. This *insouciance* (underpinned by the multicultural propaganda that has insisted that the newcomers did not really have to fully integrate into Canadian society, but were entitled, to a degree, to live according to the culture and mores of their country of origin) has translated into minuscule official systemic pressure to integrate meaningfully.

A moral contract between the newcomers and the host society would better define the mutual legitimate expectations of the two parties and spell out what each party has to contribute in order to effect the sort of reasonable accommodations that are likely to generate the newcomers' successful integration in the host society.

This is an idea that gained currency in Quebec in the early 1990s.[117] The proposed moral contract was presented as defining the mutual expectations of the different parties: not only the rights of each party, but also their obligations. Even though this moral contract has only a symbolic value, it is nevertheless a solid basis on which to redefine the set of privileges and duties. For instance, in the case of immigration, the moral contract with immigrants proposed by Gagnon-Tremblay and Cherry emphasized the expectations of the host society about the knowledge of French as an official and common language in Quebec, about the expected participation of newcomers to Quebec's development, and about the limits that the common public culture in good currency in Quebec imposes on the behaviour of citizens and, therefore, of all newcomers in Quebec and throughout Canada.

The language used was wisely kept strategically vague, but it emphasized the important valence of certain cultural and linguistic dimensions as public goods – as heritage – and it translated this valence into the duties that flow from them for the citizen. This sort of Charter-like instrument appeared to be all the more important since the Supreme Court (in the aftermath of the 1982 Charter) had ruled that governments must demonstrate that laws and regulations that they promulgate (if they have an impact on individual rights) are not only reasonable, but that such laws and regulations are necessary.[118]

---

[117] M. Gagnon-Tremblay and N. Cherry. 1990. *Au Québec pour bâtir ensemble.* Quebec: Governement de Québec.

[118] Henri Brun. June 1989. "Droits individuels et droits collectifs : un difficile équilibre," *Relations,* no. 551.

In matters that have to do with *"l'instinct de survie"* of the host society – or matters of that sort – nothing less than a moral contract or a charter of obligations and duties for newcomers (that would be a complement to the charter of rights) would appear to have the potential of not being declared *ultra vires* by the court.

# A circumspect appraisal of the state of play by officialdom

No immigration regime in the world can be regarded as some sort of *optimum optimorum*. Each regime has defendable and less defendable aspects, and each regime, of necessity, evolves through time as the environment changes and as the result of some sort of jurisprudence shifting the focus of the regime more or less importantly. This is what governance as an inquiring system ensures.

The most prudent way to assess the current Canadian issues raised by the current immigration regime is to begin with concerns that are readily conceded even by the official defenders of this regime as problematic.

We can then proceed to other matters that are more contentious and more vehemently denied, but are revealed by any critical examination of the regime by fair-minded external observers.

## *Concerns officially acknowledged*
To gauge these concerns, I have used information from an important celebratory presentation of the regime on the occasion of the Harold Crabtree Foundation Award in Public Policy Lecture at the University of Western Ontario on October 20, 2010 – not an occasion for improvisation, but one where the pronouncements have been closely scrutinized by officials.[119]

---

[119] Deborah Carson Tunis. October 21, 2010. *Fostering and Integrated Society: An Aspiration or a Reality?* Harold Crabtree Foundation Award in Public Policy Lecture at the University of Western Ontario. At the time the lecture was delivered, Deborah Carson Tunis was Director General, Integration Branch, Citizenship and Immigration Canada.

- Earnings and employment rates of recent newcomers have declined compared to the Canadian-born and more established immigrants. In 2005, immigrant men earned 63 cents for every dollar earned by a Canadian-born worker while, 25 years ago, the ratio was 85 cents. The drop is even more dramatic for immigrant women – from 85 cents to 56 cents. The incidence of low income among new immigrants is double what it is for non-immigrants.[120]

- Challenges related to cultural adaptation. It has been found that cultural adaptation is difficult when cultural norms and practices come into conflict with Canadian traditions and laws. Foreign cultural practices that violate equality rights, or are criminal offences, do not lend themselves to accommodation. There is growing concern with the possibility that some newcomers and minorities may be actively resisting integration.[121]

The words are carefully chosen, and there is always the caveat that the "absence of an empirical evidence-base on many of the issues covered under this category (the latter bullet point above) impedes an informed policy discussion,"[122] but there is an open acknowledgement that economic and cultural integration are causes for concern within Citizenship and Immigration Canada.

In addition, there is concern about the composition of this flow that encompasses only a small portion of economic immigrants appropriately screened as able to fit well into Canada's workforce. A growing number of other immigrants brought in under family reunification clauses may have neither the linguistic nor the work-related qualifications to be value-adding.

What is less clear is what will be done about these concerns.

Some suggestions about doing much more serious testing and assessments before the immigrants' arrival on Canadian

---

[120] Deborah Carson Tunis, 2010, p. 29.

[121] Deborah Carson Tunis, 2010, p. 29, 32.

[122] Deborah Carson Tunis, 2010, p. 32.

soil are encouraging, but most of the department's emphasis appears to be on improving and providing more assistance at the integration phase, without seemingly being willing to acknowledge the fact that too many unsuitable newcomers being accepted may simply mean that they are unlikely to be able to integrate well despite these efforts.

### Officially unacknowledged sources of concern

The Carson Tunis document is most revealing in its discussion of the problems that remain officially unacknowledged:

There is an unambiguous endorsement of the view that "immigration contributes to increased economic growth, innovation, entrepreneurship and competitiveness", despite all the caveats to this proposition that have been adduced to the evidence file, especially when it comes to massive and indiscriminate immigration.[123]

There is also an unambiguous restatement as gospel truth, of the supposed Canadian consensus ("accepted by most Canadians") of the very questionable assumption that "retention and fostering ethno-cultural identity was a means to encourage full participation in Canadian society."[124] Attention was drawn to the centrality of the multiculturalism commitment in defining the integrated society that is aimed at[125] thereby underlining the dogmatic commitment of the linkage between strengthening ethno-cultural identity and integration.

Despite the catalogue of documented complaints about the immigration regime, the presentation states as an unchallengeable fact that "The immigration system is trusted and valued", and validates that statement by simply noting that it was a statement endorsed in June 2010 by the federal-provincial-territorial ministers responsible for immigration – as if this pronouncement about the regime by those responsible for managing it could be interpreted as either representing the

---

[123] Deborah Carson Tunis, 2010, p. 40.
[124] Deborah Carson Tunis, 2010, p. 7.
[125] Deborah Carson Tunis, 2010, p. 40.

views of the Canadian population and experts or providing some sort of warranty that no repair is needed.[126]

More importantly perhaps, the main driver of the immigration regime is presented on page 3 of the Carson Tunis presentation as "increasing diversity" for diversity is the defining character of the country. This assumption is so central that it drives the whole presentation. It is only on page 34 of the PowerPoint presentation that we come to some strategic goals highlighting the challenges of integration, and there is only marginal reference to a commitment to a prosperous, healthy, safe and secure Canada as a driver much later in the presentation – this being given the same level of importance as management and accountability.

## Toward a new Canadian immigration regime

Governance and policy are not (as it is too often assumed) a simple game of goals and control mechanisms to reach them in a relatively stable terrain. In most non-trivial issues in social systems, the goals are ill-defined and debatable, and means-ends relationships are unstable and unreliable. Therefore, governance should not be stylized as a simple bow-arrow-target game, but seen more as putting in place an inquiring system.

An inquiring system is fundamentally about seeking and processing information as a sort of self-organized, direction-finding, super automatic pilot. It is designed to mop up information; to actively seek out anomalies and investigate identifiable pathologies; to explore problem definitions; to seek out potential collaborators; to generate prototypes of responses from conversations with those collaborators; to fail early and to fail often, using these prototypes but also to learn quickly and thoroughly from each such experimentation; to disseminate the good and bad news about what has been learned; and, to thereby close the knowing-doing gap within the organization or society.[127]

---

[126] Deborah Carson Tunis, 2010, p. 38.
[127] Gilles Paquet and Christopher Wilson, 2011.

This approach builds on intelligence and innovation – originating with an intelligence gathering function, making use of all available search processes, and being satisfied with keeping the organization of the system within a certain corridor, defined by certain norms of behaviour and acceptableness.

Governing an immigration regime aims at putting in place an assemblage of mechanisms and practices of collaboration (with crucial partners) and social learning, capable of supplementing the political process of collective decision making by affording it a capacity to avoid avoidable mistakes. In order to guide the construction of a good inquiring system, one has to acknowledge the existence of various types of migrants who need to be accommodated through somewhat different channels: standard immigrants, temporary workers, and refugees – each calling for different selection criteria, networks of partners in selecting them, terms of engagement, and expectations of integration.

What is proposed here is a substantive sample of initiatives as a basis for the necessary conversation that Canadians must have about their immigration regime. It has a strategic flavour, in the sense that it wishes to define, as a starting point, those initiatives likely to generate the least opposition, so as to build a momentum (and with it a social movement)[128] capable of undermining dominant assumptions and creating the emergent publics likely to press for a change of regime.

What is intended in the next portions of the chapter is first, to identify the families of transformations in the governance of the immigration regime that are called for; second, to specify what might be regarded as uncontroversial process changes to kick-start the social learning required; third, to gauge provisionally what might serve as a basis for the development of a moral contract with newcomers; and fourth, to suggest how terms of integration and default settings can be designed to ensure that

---

[128] Ian Angus. 2001. *Emergent Publics*. Winnipeg: Arbeiter Ring Publishing. As Angus suggests, social movements are the crucible for emergent publics that can criticize dominant social assumptions: they bring new actors on the political stage and open up the possibility for the larger population so that a change can occur.

the immigration process serves its crucial purposes – mainly to support a prosperous, healthy, safe and secure future for Canada, and secondarily, to play a humanitarian role, to the extent of Canada's absorptive capacity.

Both the repairs and the new initiatives in the governance of the immigration regime should be undertaken with a view to ensuring fairness, and in keeping with a philosophy of hospitality.

## A battery of uncontroversial initiatives

As mentioned in chapter 1, the best strategy in helping the inquiring system to improve on the present situation (without triggering an ideological war with those arguing for massive and indiscriminate immigration) is to focus on pathologies that would appear to be regarded by all Canadians as deplorable and, therefore, in need of being corrected.

Such initiatives can be introduced relatively painlessly in the short run (i.e., within one year) at the micro-level (i.e., in those portions of the immigration regime, often at the administrative level, that are in need of such repairs) but without disturbing the overall apparatus.

The Harper government has already begun to proceed in this manner (one might say) by focusing on some of the most outrageous failures of the present system: failing to find and deport criminal elements that had overstayed their welcome in the country, etc.

(a) Many of these initiatives have been explicitly put forward by the Centre for Immigration Policy Reform and its associates, and can be implemented immediately by regulation:[129]

    i) a greater insistence on the immigrants` having a working knowledge of French or English before being considered for admission to Canada;

    ii) a more critical scrutiny of the real practical value for the Canadian workplace of the education and experience of those seeking permission to immigrate;

---

[129] www.immigrationreform.ca.

iii) importance being given to the immigrant's readiness and willingness to demonstrate a cultural compatibility as well as a probability of goodness of fit with the Canadian common public culture;

iv) a limitation on family class, temporary foreign workers, and live-in caregivers; and,

v) in the case of regulated professions, immigrants should be admitted only if they are pre-qualified by the relevant authorities.

In parallel, certain administrative processes should be improved:

i) as great a proportion as possible of the prospective immigrants should be interviewed face-to-face by an immigration officer, with a view to improving the screening process; and,

ii) regulations should be modified to ensure that marriage frauds are eliminated, by limiting spousal sponsorship to couples married or living together for at least two years before sponsorship applications are commenced, and that only the children of permanent residents would automatically receive Canadian citizenship.

(b) A large number of questions have been raised about a variety of specific programs dealing with particular groups (temporary workers, live-in caregivers, entrepreneurs and business persons, etc.). In all cases, the negative evidence is important enough to suggest abolishing, scaling back or reforming seriously such programs, or imposing much tighter regulations to prevent abuse.

It should be announced that all such programs will be subjected within the next year to a very critical review, and that in the future any such special program will have a built-in requirement of a full evaluative review every five years.

(c) It would be politically unpalatable to proclaim and announce an arbitrarily reduced number as the new total annual inflow of newcomers into Canada. It would simply perpetuate the era of whimsicality. But it is not unreasonable for the government to suggest its intention, after the current consultation with Canadians about the size and mix of annual immigration inflows into Canada, to declare formally that the future size of annual immigration flows will be in keeping with Canada's absorptive capacity. In the meantime, the planned annual immigration flow of standard immigrants in these times of high economic uncertainty should be reduced below the present level, as a result of the tightening of selection criteria, and ensuring that the mix of immigrants pegged at 75 percent economic, 10 percent family, 15 percent refugees or something of the sort.

Many initiatives might require a revision of the *Immigration and Refugee Protection Act* (IRPA) and of the *Canadian Citizenship Act* (CCA). Such modifications cannot be made hurriedly, but should be planned over the next three years. Indeed, this should be the occasion to build into the law a need to critically review these acts every decade.

In parallel, a wide variety of administrative regulatory measures could be announced – to be introduced as soon as possible – when changes in regulations would suffice:

  i) a permanent resident smart identity card should ensure a reasonable tracking and monitoring of residency and adherence to residency requirements by those applying for citizenship; and,

  ii) a decision to require tax filing from Canadian citizens, wherever they are, with the possibility of the citizenship being revoked if there is a failure to file for five years.

### Some not very controversial process repairs

There are modifications to the Canadian immigration and refugee regimes that can be regarded as not very controversial if they are clearly explained, their rationale made plain and understandable to all as fair and reasonable, so that there can be no misunderstanding about the Canadian philosophy on such matters.

(a) Quantitatively, immigration levels should be modulated according to the economic and employment circumstances of the country: more immigrants in good times, and fewer in bad times.

(b) Qualitatively, it should be clear that there are two streams entering the country: those immigrants who are selected on the basis of characteristics that prepare them to fit within the country well (language and other skills); and then those who are admitted to the country on humanitarian and compassionate grounds (refugee, family class). Both streams should be modulated according to the absorptive capacity of the country and as the result of an appreciation of the economic and employment circumstances, but also of the likelihood of the immigrants fitting well into Canadian society.

(c) In the selection of standard immigrants, it should be clear that not requiring a modicum of linguistic and work skills is bound to condemn the newcomers to serious difficulties in integrating within the Canadian workforce. Therefore, from now on, evaluation of the suitability of the regular immigrants should not be allowed to proceed (barring particular circumstances) without a face-to-face meeting with an immigration officer charged with assessing the candidates on the basis of these skills, and of their capacity to adapt to Canadian ways.

(d) In matters of family class immigration, it should be established that reunification would apply only to immediate family, i.e., spouses and unmarried, dependent minor children, and that linguistic, security and health conditions may apply.

(e) With reference to refugees, a limit on the number of refugees to be admitted each year should be established, and priority should be given to the refugees living in United Nations-sponsored camps. A rigorous process of evaluation should allow Canada to evaluate health and security risks before anyone is admitted. People who arrive from safe third countries should not be allowed to make refugee claims. The process should ensure a final decision on claims within weeks, not years.

(f) Acquisition and maintenance of citizenship should be tightened (1) by increasing the waiting period from three to five years for a permanent resident to apply for citizenship (as was formerly the case); (2) by ending the practice of granting automatic citizenship to a child born in Canada of non-Canadian parents, in line with the policies in Australia, New

Zealand, Britain, and other European countries; (3) by denying access to social services, such as the public health care system – to Canadian citizens who have chosen to live abroad for extended periods, unless they have continuously contributed through their income taxes to the financing of these programs; and (4) by clearly establishing that holders of Canadian passports who have chosen to live abroad for very extended periods cannot expect to receive anything but consular assistance in times of difficulty.[130]

## The moral contracts with newcomers

Other modifications to the immigration and refugee regimes are likely to be more controversial because they would be based on a refurbished and strengthened notion of citizenship. As was noted earlier, a meaningful notion of citizenship is based on an understanding that an immigrant is not simply entering a bingo hall when he or she comes to Canada, but is joining our society as a matter of privilege.

In the documentation made available to potential immigrants, the newcomer should be fully informed about the expectations that the host country clearly asserts as the *quid pro quo* for all the support services and entitlements that are afforded to the newcomer.[131] Moreover, it should be made as clear as possible, in an adequate briefing, that immigrants are expected to adapt to the common public culture, and exactly what services newcomers will be afforded to help them meet the terms of adjustment and integration to the culture and norms of the host country.

---

[130] Situations of this sort have led to the development of unreasonable expectations on the part of such 'casual Canadians.' See Andrew Cohen. 2007. *The Unfinished Canadian*. Toronto: McClelland & Stewart, chapter 5.

[131] A number of Western countries have been developing extensive briefing programs to give to prospective newcomers a very accurate picture of what to expect should they decide to make the move. The purpose of such briefings is explicitly to discourage those persons and their families who are likely to have serious problems in adapting to the cultural norms and practices of the receiving country (Martin Collacott. 2008. "Has it become too easy to acquire Canadian citizenship?" *Canadian Diversity*, 6(4): 141-144).

## The evolving common public culture of the host society as ground zero

In a pluralist society, there are no shared values.[132] Through their life experience, individuals and groups develop different values and identities,[133] but they have to negotiate some agreement about a variety of norms and principles to coordinate their activities in daily life. Gary Caldwell has used the notion of **common public culture** to encompass the concrete expression of the ensemble of rules of the game on which such an agreement has been reached – (1) from codes and conventions of politeness and *savoir-vivre*; (2) to the rules of the game proper (freedoms, rights, responsibilities, virtues); (3) to basic principles like the rule of law or the separation of church and state; and (4) to essential beliefs like freedom of choice and equality of men and women.[134] As Caldwell suggests, the first two layers are *grosso modo* the **rules of the social game**; the last two are the **foundations** on which these are built.

This baroque ensemble is obviously not static. Over time, it will evolve as a result of experience and social learning. The death penalty used to be part of the rules of the game in Canada, but it has been determined over the last while that it was no longer a valid rule. Generally speaking, one can best describe this ensemble as a corpus of **conventions** that are more or less deeply grounded and, therefore, can be regarded as more or less deeply ingrained in a society's way of life. One would expect all these conventions to evolve over time as a result of discussion within the society, but also as a result of the growing awareness and understanding of the benefits and costs of all sorts attached to them, and the transformation they bring about in the very fabric of that society.

Clearly, the top two layers of this ensemble may be regarded as more easily negotiable (though it may not be easy)

---

[132] Joseph Heath. 2003. *The Myth of Shared Values in Canada*. Ottawa: Canadian Centre for Management Development.

[133] George A. Akerlof and Rachel E. Kranton. 2010. *Identity Economics*. Princeton: Princeton University Press.

[134] Gary Caldwell. 2001. *La culture publique commune*. Quebec: Éditions Nota Bene, chapter 3.

than the foundational ones. Such negotiation may be more or less difficult, depending on the extent to which these different conventions have come to be regarded as essential to the identity of the group, or somewhat peripheral, or simply as a matter of temporary fashion.

For instance, in the process of transmission of culture some aspects of the mores may evolve quickly, like the wearing of some types of hat or gloves, or the use of *vous* and *tu* in different circumstances. Other aspects, having to do with codes of honour, may, on the other hand, truly require moral revolutions to be modified, and may not only take more time, but be very difficult to carry out, even when the costs of maintaining the old ways may be regarded as enormously high.[135]

When newcomers request the privilege of joining the host society, they have to accept the idea that they are entering a complex and delicate set of arrangements that cannot be disturbed without consequences. Some of these arrangements may ostensibly be visible, but may not constitute something that is particularly cherished. Cohabitation of different ways of life may then be regarded as quite acceptable and, even in a relatively short time, become part of the refurbished common public culture. Others may be cherished for reasons that are not clear to the newcomer and quickly become a source of tension when they are challenged. Indeed, some may be icons representing fundamental aspects of a way of life that the host society regards as quintessential and not negotiable at all.

It would be great if all this baroque ensemble of conventions were clearly and unequivocally defined, and if the degree of non-negotiability of each one was well known to all. It would also be great if the newcomer were to join the host society unburdened by any cultural baggage of his/her own. Such is not the world we live in.

There is much that is latent and unspoken in the host society's common public culture, and any newcomer carries

---

[135] K. Anthony Appiah. 2010. *The Honor Code – How Moral Revolutions Happen.* New York: W.W. Norton.

with him/her many conventions originating from another society where the common public culture may be quite different.

The only reasonable basis for viable accommodation between these different common public cultures is for the newcomer to ascertain as fully as possible the nature of the common public culture of the host society, and to determine if he/she can accommodate to it. If, for instance, a newcomer were to join a host society while firmly believing and stating clearly that he/she considers (1) the members of the host society as 'dogs' unworthy of any consideration, and (2) that their usages and mores are globally depraved and to be opposed *in toto*, one might reasonably suggest that this is a bad fit, and that the newcomer should consider joining another sort of club.

However, it should also be clear from our earlier discussion that not all aspects of the common public culture of the host society are equally non-negotiable. The reality of **reasonable accommodation** is the determination of the extent to which the newcomer will have to adapt to the different sets of arrangements in good currency in the host society: either totally, in good part, or not necessarily.

But it should also be clear that, if the newcomer wants the privilege of joining the host society, he/she has to agree to shoulder most of the accommodation to the common public culture in the host society. This is the view held by 70 percent of Canadians, but not the view arrived at by the officialdom of the Bouchard-Taylor Commission in Quebec. Rather, the commission has suggested that the bulk of the accommodation has to be shouldered by the host society. This explains why the commission report was summarily shelved: it was in too sharp a contradiction with the views of the citizenry.

Consequently, one needs to start with the host society's common public culture as ground zero, as the starting point for negotiations between the host society and the newcomers.

## Negotiating moral contracts[136]

Native-born citizens have legitimate expectations that some of the trust and social capital that have been built over generations will not and should not be dissipated lightly; newcomers have legitimate expectations that there will be some accommodation to take into account some of their needs and preferences, since they intend to make a value-adding contribution to the host society.

As the assumptions on which the host community is based are challenged by newcomers (sometimes seemingly with a righteous sense that there is no limit to legitimate demands for a displacement of the host society's principles and institutions), there may be a reflex closing of the mind to the demands of the new groups; and as the demands of the new citizens are denied, a growing sense of alienation and exclusion among the newcomers is bound to ensue. As a result, the two groups may become mutually antagonistic and collaboration may become more and more difficult. We know that the economic, social and political costs of such antagonism are large.

Dealing with this conundrum requires that the problem of moral distrust be engaged directly. Most of the time, this is not resolvable through the orthopaedic interventions of the law, but requires negotiated soft arrangements, like moral contracts, that establish the basis for the definition of mutual expectations.

For many reasons, the challenge of negotiating such moral contracts is daunting.

First, such negotiation entails a clarification of expectations on both sides that may not at first appear as unduly constraining (one can imagine a wide range of moral contracts, more or less binding on both established and new citizens) but, to the extent that culture means anything, this is an arduous task: it means a capacity to recognize differences, to accomplish some integration of these differences, and to succeed in determining some hierarchy

---

[136] The following paragraphs borrow freely from Gilles Paquet. 2008. *Deep Cultural Diversity – A Governance Challenge*. Ottawa: University of Ottawa Press, chapter 7.

in this more or less diversified and more or less integrated complex of principles.[137]

Second, the very informality of these 'contractual' arrangements leaves them open not only to genuine misinterpretation, but also to sabotage by those intent on using this very vagueness to pursue other political or electoral objectives. Indeed, deception is the Achilles heel of moral contracts. The systematic misuse of the language of the Charter and of human rights legislation to camouflage one's own preferences or desires into entitlements and imperatives has provided much evidence of the usage of deception in aid of ideological pursuits.

Moral contracts are meant not only to establish guidelines on what the newcomers may expect, but also to set limits to the level of diversity accommodation that a society regards as legitimate. This latter level of tolerance will often depend on certain basic tenets of the host society that it feels incapable of abandoning for fear that it would not be capable of withstanding the anomie-generating pressures emerging from a no-limit diversity stance that would not protect such tenets. Both constraints and limits would be determined through some **principle of precedence:**[138] some constraints being regarded as taking precedence over others in the definition of viable arrangements. Deep diversity cannot be managed otherwise.

### A plausible point of departure

Nowhere is there a clear mapping of the terrain where accommodation can or cannot be negotiated. Gary Caldwell[139] has prudently surveyed the terrain but has been reluctant to determine whether crucial tangible borders might exist

---

[137] Bruno Lussato. 1989. *Le défi culturel.* Paris: Nathan.

[138] David Braybrooke. 1987. *Meeting Needs.* Princeton: Princeton University Press.

[139] Gary Caldwell, 2001. Caldwell has just published a modified version of the 2001 book in English for a pan-Canadian public (Gary Caldwell. 2012. *Canadian Public Culture – The rules of the game in Canadian public life and their justification.* St-Edwidge, QC: Fermentation Press).

between what is negotiable and not negotiable. Yet, this is an issue that requires immediate attention because, even if in the longer run this may change, it is not possible to engage newcomers in a meaningful conversation unless one is able at the very least to identify a plausible list of some of the items that would appear, in the short run, to be non-negotiable.

A complete review of the whole array of conventions (covering the whole range from etiquette to freedoms, rights, responsibilities, to principles and beliefs) might be both tedious and fraught with immense difficulties, at least until one has clarified some foundational basic principles and essential beliefs that would appear to underpin the common public culture.

As a preliminary step, I have taken the bold move of producing a minimal list (drawing much from the lists proposed by Caldwell) under each of the two more fundamental rubrics he has used, in order to present a plausible set of principles or beliefs about which a broad consensus might be generated.

| Basic principles | Essential beliefs |
| --- | --- |
| Representative democracy | Freedom of choice |
| Separation of church from state | Equality of opportunity |
| Rule of law | Equality of men and women |
| Responsibility for one's actions | Collaboration |
| Duty to help those in need | Fraternity |

These lists are not presented as self-evident, but as examples of principles and beliefs that might be of help in determining what is and is not negotiable in the moral contracts with the newcomers. It should be clear that while, in practice, one may fail to live up to these principles and beliefs, they would appear to correspond to a plausible set that might approximate a sort of hard core of the common public culture that may be defendable.

This sample of principles and beliefs is itself open to debate, and should indeed be debated in due course. But for the immediate purposes of discussion, let us assume that until these sets have been disputed and dislodged from such a position (representing the defendable outcome of a long common experience that has led a community to develop such an anchor), they may be regarded as **temporary reference points** in determining what is not negotiable.

In such a case, any person violently opposed to these principles and beliefs might find it difficult to live within the community. And to the extent that such principles and beliefs are regarded by the community as foundational, accommodation becomes problematic. Consequently, if newcomers were to feel incapable of accepting these principles and beliefs, and were to declare that they would not only challenge them but forcefully fight at them, it is clear that it would not be unreasonable to ask whether the host society wishes to grant to such individuals the privilege of joining this community.

Again, in a pluralist society, agreement on any such set of beliefs and principles does not mean that all persons need to have the same values. Some may regard these principles and beliefs as echoing their most profound values indeed, while others may simply accept them as convenient contraptions. But one might expect that they would be the outcome of some legitimate discussion.

Once it has been established that there exists a core common public culture that is intensely appreciated by the host society, it becomes fair to ask to what extent it is desirable and legitimate for the host society to ensure itself that this common public culture will not be undermined by inviting into the host society elements determined to overthrow it.

For instance, how wise is it for a liberal society to accept in its midst illiberal elements determined to undermine and overthrow its liberal regime? How wise is it for a society that is based on the separation of church and state, and has a strong belief in fraternity, to allow indiscriminate massive immigration by elements that believe that the state should be subservient to the church, and that citizens who are not members of their faith are and should be treated as 'dogs'?

It would appear reasonable that, in the screening of newcomers, it should be established beyond a reasonable doubt that they incontrovertibly and honestly accept the obligation to live by the core principles and beliefs in good currency in the host society, such as those sketched above, as well as by the rules and codes that would appear to follow from them.

One may argue that anyone who is not willing to accept the full equality of men and women, to accept the need to have a command of the *lingua franca*, to be a fully responsible producer of governance, and to display the willingness to operate *à visage découvert* with other fraternal citizens, might be regarded as unfit to be granted the privilege of joining the host society. *A fortiori*, anyone involved in actively undermining these principles and beliefs, despite having been clearly informed that they are non-negotiable conditions of admission, would be regarded as *persona non grata*.

There is no reason why there should not be an ongoing conversation about the evolution of rules and conventions to accommodate newcomers (within the constraint of the agreed set of core principles and beliefs) and even an ongoing conversation about how the set of core principles and beliefs regarded as in good currency in a given society might evolve consensually. Indeed, this is what is ideally happening in the forum in liberal societies. But as the newcomers join the host society, accepting the core principles and beliefs in place at the time of entry is a *sine qua non*, and this would of necessity constrain the democratic negotiation of the moral contracts, defining the mutual expectations of the host society and of the newcomers in the short run.

Moreover, these imperatives can be expected to shape the immigration and refugee regimes accordingly.

Much of this negotiation work must be done to ensure that the foundations of fraternity and solidarity in the host society are not eroded, and it would explicitly factor solidarity and security as elements that need to be taken into account in deciding how many and whom to admit to the host society.

# Terms of integration and default settings

Working at designing an immigration regime cannot be limited to considerations of gate-keeping.

The immigration regime must deal explicitly with the terms of engagement and integration regarded as workable by the host society. These rules are for the time being very ill-defined, as a result of the shadow of multiculturalism. If the diversity imperative and the multiculturalist ideology were to continue to prevail unchallenged, terms of engagement and integration would be bound to be immensely light: the myth of the equality of all cultures would prevail and, consequently, one cannot easily envisage what conditions one might legitimately impose on the newcomers (except that of not openly violating the law) that could not be challenged in the courts.

It is therefore important, in order to escape from the *chape de plomb* of multiculturalism and to pave the way to reasonable accommodation – that the terms of engagement and integration be couched in the form of moral contracts that would have Charter-like status.

This might proceed in two complementary ways.

First, one might start with a rough reconciliation of the moral contracts more or less in existence as a reflection of the present arrangements that have acquired legitimacy. This might be difficult in Canada since much of the accommodation has been left to the local level,[140] and that there might be some variability across the country. But the occasion of the impending review of key legislation on immigration and refugee protection and on citizenship might provide an opportunity to put forward a rough approximate prototype of the foundations for the moral contract that might serve to kick start the conversation. This rough reconciliation of present practices in the first instance could develop though jurisprudence over time.

It is crucial that a multi-logue on such a question is initiated on the occasion of the review of the *Immigration and Refugee Protection Act* (IRPA) and the *Citizenship Act* (CA), and that the

---

[140] Raymond Breton. 2003. "Societal Governance and Increasing Ethnic Diversity," *www.optimumonline.ca*, 33(1): 9-12.

revised versions of these laws refer to (1) some prototype of the moral contract echoing some broad version of kernel beliefs and principles guiding the definition of what rules and conventions are not negotiable; (2) some safe-fail mechanisms to ensure that the evolving moral contract is protected from sabotage by mischievous uses of the Charter; and, (3) some mechanisms of review of these rules and conventions over time – maybe every 10 years.

This may require, in a world that has shown little courage on this front, that such moral contracts be referred to in the documentation giving the newcomer permission to immigrate, together with a precise statement about the monitoring to be expected, and the consequences of not abiding by the moral contracts at the time when a decision about citizenship is to be arrived at. If newcomers must agree ahead of time with the terms of engagement and integration in good currency in Canada, it should be deemed to apply to anyone setting foot on Canadian soil, and it would prevent a replay of the Singh fiasco of the 1980s.

The vagueness and diffuse character of this sort of definition of mutual expectations may appear to some as unworkable as a basis for accommodation and collaboration. That is not the case. In French corporate law, this sort of spirit of collaboration has a name – *affectio societatis*.[141] It entails that active and creative contribution of all parties to a partnership is expected as part of a postulated moral contract. Failure to demonstrate *affectio societatis* may lead to the dissolution of the partnership. Experience has proved that it has become a foundational aspect of French law, and has turned out to be more operational than it might at first have appeared.

Second, the moral contracts can only work if, as part of the conditions of admission to membership, they are well explained, both to the newcomers as part of the fair and legitimate rules of hospitality, but are also well known to all in the host society. This entails an important education of the citizenry in order for them to take ownership of these principles, beliefs, rules and conventions that are supposed to have their support. This is crucial, especially in preparation for the eventuality of persons not living up to these commitments and being asked to leave.[142]

Up to now, clear violations of the precise terms of engagement and integration are too often met with a romantic compassion that amounts to an invalidation of the rules arrived at in the name of fair play and reasonable hospitality. There is a long list of organizations that, in the name of indiscriminate compassion, are willing to take on the crusade to exempt X or Y or Z from such clear rules. This attaches much odium to enforcing clear and legitimate rules, and explains why there has been such laxity in executing deportation orders, even in the case of known criminals.

Consequently, much has to be done to ensure that default settings are put in place in the admission and integration process to immunize them from fanciful appeals, as well as from unreasonable and costly delays in executing orders, following from conditions of presence in the country or conditions for citizenship not being met.

Episodes like the events in the summer of 2006, when between 40 and 50 thousand persons holding Canadian

---

[142] As this book is going to press, one is reminded starkly that the imperfect intergenerational transmission of the common public culture may create difficulties in the negotiation of moral contracts with newcomers. For instance, one can hardly insist on the basic principle of the rule of law being respected by newcomers when it is flouted by young (and not so young) Canadians *de souche*. Recent events in Quebec are a source of concern. Injunctions served by tribunals, to order schools to provide courses for students who have decided not to boycott them, were not executed by school officials as a result of intimidation and violence perpetrated by groups of students defending the boycott, even though these groups have no right to do such things (Andrew Coyne. 2012. "For Quebec students, might makes right," *Ottawa Citizen*, May 10, A13). Not upholding the basic principle of the rule of law is an omen of much social disorder to come, and yet it has been tolerated. All this points to the central importance of restating these principles for segments of the Canadian-born citizenry, but also of the governments, when they would appear to have lapsed into ignoring them: this is crucial if one is to be allowed to present them legitimately to newcomers as basic principles to which they have to adhere.

passports were in Lebanon and demanded to be repatriated, are cautionary tales. Some 'accidental tourists,' but also a very large number of 'casual Canadians' (many of whom had paid no tax in Canada for decades), demanded that the Canadian government accept responsibility for their return to Canada. Even though some $96 million was spent on this operation, there was nothing but a catalogue of complaints about the embassy not answering calls, dirty boats, overflowing toilets, scarce food, choppy seas, etc.[143]

Unlimited expectations were allowed to be regarded as legitimate, the government of Canada was barked at by 'citizens of convenience' (with the sanctimonious support of the media), and bizarre polls in Canada were showing that eight of ten Canadians felt that they had a right to expect the government to evacuate them from a dangerous area.

Unless duties and expectations are more clearly agreed to in advance, citizenship is simply a licence to express unlimited entitlements while acknowledging no duties. It should be a key component of the review of the IRPA and of the CA to define more clearly default settings spelling out what citizens of convenience can expect from the Canadian government in situations of the sort.

But it is not sufficient to refer to such extreme situations. One must also expect from such refurbished laws that they will define default settings for ordinary times as well. In the absence of clear notions of conditionality, expectations are allowed to become grossly inflated and, given the tendency for Canadians to want to look decent, diligent and kind to a fault, unless such default settings are brutally clear, much abuse will ensue.

## Conclusion

What about the numbers? This is one of the crucial concerns of those who think that Canada is unwittingly allowing its common public culture to be eroded because of excessive

---

[143] Andrew Cohen, 2007, p. 145ff.

immigration – an immigration flow that is larger than the country can absorb.

It is my view that numbers should be the outcome of the refurbished immigration regime, rather than the driver of it. If the various processes mentioned above (in particular at the selection level) were to be modified in light of the laws of hospitality and fair play, in keeping with Canada's absorptive capacity and the obligation to preserve the common public culture, there would be a significant decline in immigration flows over the middle run (i.e., over the next few years) – back to the pre-1990 average level, maybe. It would be the result, not of a *guerre des chiffres*, but of a general tightening of the conditions of entry, of the conditions of membership, and of the terms of engagement and integration.

As to the share of the total that should be allotted to different types of migrants, again it would probably evolve in the direction favoured by the Centre on Immigration Policy Reform (75 percent economic, 10 percent family reunification, 15 percent refugees), but it would be as a result not of whims but of basic principles being allowed to be at play, and it would probably mean a different sort of person being considered as eligible (especially on the refugee front) when humanitarian priorities might force the officials, in the first instance, to focus on refugees already parked in United Nations refugee camps.

All this may take a few years, if the nexus of issues making up the immigration regime is firmly tackled now. Any attempt to more quickly right the wrongs of a disastrous policy that has been in good currency for some 25 years (and that has, in the meantime, created a fair number of interest groups) might prove hazardous and perilous.

This will probably not satisfy those who fear that the economic, social, security and cultural impacts of the current regime may create irreversible damage to the country, and who call for draconian action immediately. To them, I can only argue that obliquity, in the circumstances, is the preferred route, and that the desired objectives will be best achieved indirectly.[144]

This does not mean that numbers should be banned from conversations about immigration, but only that they should be de-fetishized. In the broad range of partners involved in the immigration regime, the federal government has a responsibility to act as a coxswain responsible for the safety of the crew. Annual numbers should be regarded as nothing more than useful signals to help coordinate the efforts of all as best as possible, while taking into account the full complement of circumstances.

Such signals should be derived from as full an appreciation as possible of the many dimensions discussed above, but always inspired by the precautionary principle.[145] This is the way matters were handled from the early 1950s to the late 1980s (with provisions to make drastic adjustments for special circumstances) and both Canada and newcomers benefited. It might be wise to return to this absorptive capacity philosophy that would fit most of the principles mentioned above.

[144] John Kay. 2011. *Obliquity*. New York: The Penguin Press.

[145] The precautionary principle is arguing that one should take pre-emptive precautions even in the absence of already existing entirely persuasive evidence when what is envisaged is the possibility of catastrophic and irreversible damage, and that the lack of full scientific certainty should not be used as a reason for postponing cost-effective measures that might help to prevent the probability of worst-case scenarios.

# | Conclusion

*"...cognitive capacity shuts down in the absence of a story..."*
*— Robyn Dawes*

The centerpiece in the morality play about massive and indiscriminate immigration in Canada over the last decades is the manufactured consensus that has been concatenated in the post-Charter era. This 'consensus' has been in the nature of "silence means consent", and has been used by analysts to propose that the current immigration regime had the support of Canadians. It is my view that this 'consensus' has been fabricated by continuous disinformation about immigration, massive government propaganda in support of the view that diversity is an absolute social good, and that all cultures are equally worthy. Therefore diversity (generated by massive immigration beyond the absorptive capacity of the country) has trumped concerns about security and solidarity, and the preservation of the common public culture has been allowed to be spirited away as a concern altogether.

This regime has been criticized aptly, but it has not been undermined because of the protective belt generated by the Charter of Rights and Freedom, political correctness, and the toxic effect of the uncritical attitudes of the intelligentsia and the media. Indeed, the intelligentsia may be considered as complicit in this hoodwinking exercise; it has supplied the rationale for what can only be regarded as an irresponsible immigration regime. From the Berry-Taylor-Kymlicka enterprise to the

Bouchard-Taylor Commission, to the Reitz sacralization of the reversal of opinions about immigration (as revealed in the polls) as a result of some untainted organic process, the intelligentsia has not only underpinned the current immigration regime, but has defended as legitimate the view that the common public culture of the host society should give way to quasi-unbounded accommodation in the name of the equality of all cultures, and the view that the newcomers should be fully accommodated.

A provisional outline of the general directions that should be pursued in developing an alternative to the current immigration regime has been sketched. However, the task before us has proved more complex than simply replacing one set of whimsical targets by another. As suggested, it has become obvious to most observers that to challenge the current immigration regime (including the 'consensus' and the ideology in good currency that underpins it), one has to proceed in two steps: first, to deconstruct the ideology and 'consensus' and provide a more reasoned and legitimate alternative cosmology; and second, to put in place the foundations of an inquiring system likely to lead to a more reasonable immigration regime.

Chapter 3 has sketched the basis of an alternative cosmology (rooted in fair play, hospitality, and reasonable accommodation) to replace the one in good currency – rooted in unbounded entitlements and imaginary rights. This has served as a platform to define the basic philosophy that should guide the new principled immigration regime described at the beginning of chapter 4.

The latter part of chapter 4 established the contours of the sort of inquiring system likely to generate the new immigration regime. This inquiring system represents a much more effective way to deal with public policy. It recognizes that public policy is, most of the time, unable to deal with wicked problems as a bow-and-arrow target game: goals and objectives are too vague and ill-defined, information is missing, means-ends relationships are unstable and unreliable and, therefore, unintended consequences are immensely more important than willed results. The best one can do is to put in place an inquiring system capable of fast social learning and constant adjustment to new circumstances. Such an inquiring system does not short-circuit the process of intelligence and innovation, but rather, in order to be more effective, proceeds through experiments and often with obliquity – avoiding unhelpful confrontations with powerful interest groups.

What has been suggested in the latter part of chapter 4 is a strategic process of inquiry and reform that is meant to refurbish the immigration regime in a matter of years. Attempting to do it more abruptly may generate more damage than good. The population has been subjected for some 30 years to propaganda that needs to be countered by exposure to a large number of anomalies that can be corrected, before the cosmology in good currency can be effectively undermined.

If one is to be successful, it is mandatory to begin with micro-interventions on technical fronts that reveal clearly unacceptable anomalies and where correctives cannot be subjected to twisted misinterpretations as racist or bigoted. If the integrity of the immigration regime is to be rescued, the process of decontamination of the public mind needs to work in such a way that those initiatives are clearly seen by the public as reasonable and necessary. It is only when such technical micro-initiatives have been successfully completed, that more ambitious reviews of special programs at the meso-level can be undertaken with general public support, and with little likelihood that powerful interest groups can distort their intent and impact to fuel ideological wars.

Such micro- and meso-reforms will have a significant impact on the flows of immigration without an outright war between cosmologies. The results may not be as dramatic as some impatient observers would like, but they will be carried out as a process that has the support of the public. Only when such meso-reforms have shown their positive results should they be 'summarized,' so to speak, in formally announced macro-numerical benchmarks – such as the total maximum annual inflows, or statements about the numerical composition of the immigration flows – as nothing more or less than a coordinating signal of the coxswain to the crew of partners in the name of the precautionary principle

Such an *étapiste* process, accompanied by constant adjustments as more is learned about the evolving dynamics of immigration, is more promising than a more brutal and confrontational one.

These initiatives appear to me to be necessary, but they are unlikely to be sufficient.

Two other important initiatives have to be developed in parallel: a credible story, and some modifications to our code of honour.

Public policy in an open pluralist society has an important preceptoral component. The citizenry is entitled to have an explanation for what is going on, an explanation that the citizens will find understandable and acceptable. Over the last while, politicians and the media have found it easier to surf on politically correct sentiments than to explain those issues in cogent terms. And the intelligentsia has found that 'progressive' tales, with their indiscriminate compassion and sentimentality, present an easier challenge than efforts to uncover the complex dynamics of social issues. What is needed is a clear storyline, defining a responsible immigration regime as one that is generous but conditional: the host society being able to impose conditions that will ensure its common public culture, a way of life developed over time, and protect its security and solidarity from being eroded.

Such a clear storyline is best built on the obverse of multiculturalism – intermediate cosmopolitanism. Multi-culturalism proposes to establish connection through building stronger separate identity claims. Cosmopolitanism presumes that connection is not through hardening identities, but despite difference. It builds on the fact that all persons have a negative duty toward other human beings (not to do harm), but may have 'thicker' relationships to closer associates. So, it tends to recognize that one has obligations to others and can learn from them, but that diversity need not be revered to the point of eroding the common public culture, or at the price of individual autonomy.[146] Such a cosmopolitan storyline has not been told, but it must be told if the notion of cosmopolitanism is to shed the connotation of 'rootlessness' and 'footlooseness' that is attached to it, and if it is to replace multiculturalism as a foundation for the new immigration regime.

But a story of "rooted intermediate cosmopolitanism" will not be sufficient for the new cosmology to take hold. As Anthony Appiah has shown,[147] what might be required in addition for the story to have an impact, and for major social transformations to be effected – like the abolition of duelling or slavery – is nothing less than a moral revolution – i.e., a large change in a short time that involves a rapid transformation of moral behaviour. And Appiah observed that, in such moral revolutions, something called "honour" plays a central role, a change in the notion of what is honourable and dishonourable.

The bare bones of the Appiah argument go as follows: a code of honour defines what is expected and regarded as honourable behaviour for an individual of a certain identity or status. Attached to the status or identity of a professional is a sort of behaviour that is regarded as honourable and, therefore, is expected. For instance, it is only if there is a change in the notion of what is honourable for a professional that one can expect a change in professional behaviour and, therefore, a change in the social arrangements that rule the profession.

The move from a culture of entitlements (and dishonour claimed when entitlements are not met) to a culture of accommodation and fair play (and honour attached to succeeding in negotiating *"la paix des braves"*) is a move away from the absoluteness of rights (a matter of **either-or**), to the contingency of the terms of engagement depending on circumstances (a matter of **more-or-less**).

[146] Gilles Paquet. 2008. *Deep Cultural Diversity – A Governance Challenge*. Ottawa: University of Ottawa Press, p. 81ff; K. Anthony Appiah. 2005. *The Ethics of Identity*. Princeton: Princeton University Press, chapter 6; K. Anthony Appiah. 2006. *Cosmopolitanism*. New York: W.W. Norton.

[147] K. Anthony Appiah. 2010. *The Honor Code – How Moral Revolutions Happen*. New York: W.W. Norton.

Fifty years of programming by the rights ideology, and 30 years of drumming identity politics and multiculturalism into the citizenry have left a deep imprint... as have 50 years of regarding policy as a simple game of bow-arrow-target. What is required now is a revolution of the mind. Some have labelled this reframing as the passage from naïve common sense to uncommon sense:[148] this entails that so-called planners agree to become 'searchers' – persons who do not know the answer in advance and hope to find the answers to individual problems by trial and error,[149] by bootstrapping (i.e., by focusing on concrete solutions to local problems, "sniffing out not only what is working, but also what could work if certain impediments were removed, constraints lifted, or problems solved elsewhere in the system").[150]

I have argued earlier that rights ideology, multiculturalism, identity politics, and the goal-and-control notion of public policy are now being clearly challenged, and that the culture of entitlements has shown its toxic impact on society. Yet the new cosmology built around rooted cosmopolitanism, reasonable accommodation, fair play and hospitality, and experimentalism in policy-making through inquiring systems has not jelled yet, and it cannot be expected to jell until special circumstances begin to reveal the full extent to which the old cosmology has been immensely toxic.

It may turn out that such circumstances are beginning to emerge on the immigration front and that the inquiring system we suggest will learn fast enough to recast the immigration regime before the worst-case scenarios materialize and leave all parties worse off. My hopes on this front are as great as the fears of some of my colleagues.

---

[148] Duncan J. Watts. 2011. *Everything is Obvious...Once You Know the Answer.* New York: Random House.

[149] William Easterly. 2006. *The White Man's Burden: Why the West's Efforts to Aid the Rest Have Done So Much Ill and So Little Good.* New York: Penguin, p. 6.

[150] Duncan J. Watts, 2011; Charles F. Sabel. 2007. "Bootstrapping Development" in V. Nee and R. Swedberg (eds.). *On Capitalism.* Palo Alto, CA: Stanford University Press.

# | References

S ome segments of this book have been previously published in a somewhat different form.

Paquet, Gilles. 2010. "Immigration and the Solidarity-Diversity-Security Nexus," *www.optimumonline.ca*, 40(4): 73-93.

Paquet, Gilles. 2011. "About Dumbfounding Aspects of Canadian Immigration Policy." Paper presented at a roundtable organized for the 45th Annual Meeting of the Canadian Economics Association held in June 2011. Published in *www. optimumonline.ca*, 41(3): 10-21.

# Titles in the Collaborative Decentred Metagovernance Series

1.  Ruth Hubbard, Gilles Paquet and
    Christopher Wilson                                          2012
    *Stewardship: Collaborative Decentred Metagovernance
    and Inquiring Systems*

2.  Gilles Paquet                                               2012
    *Moderato cantabile: Toward Principled Governance
    for Canada's Immigration Policy*

## Other titles published by INVENIRE

12. Richard Clément et Caroline Andrew (sld)                   2012
    *Villes et langues : gouvernance et politiques
    Symposium international*

11. Richard Clément and Caroline Andrew (eds)                  2012
    *Cities and Languages: Governance and Policy
    International Symposium*

10. Michael Behiels and François Rocher (eds)                  2011
    *The State in Transition: Challenges for
    Canadian Federalism*

9.  Pierre Camu                                                 2011
    *La Flotte Blanche : Histoire de la Compagnie de
    Navigation du Richelieu et d'Ontario, 1845-1913*

8.  Rupak Chattopadhyay and Gilles Paquet (eds)               2011
    *The Unimagined Canadian Capital:
    Challenges for the Federal Capital Region*

7.  Gilles Paquet                                              2011
    *Tableau d'avancement II : Essais exploratoires sur la
    gouvernance d'un certain Canada français*

6.  James Bowen (ed)                                           2011
    *The Entrepreneurial Effect: Waterloo*

5.  François Lapointe                                          2011
    *Cities as Crucibles: Reflections on Canada's
    Urban Future*

4.  James Bowen (ed)                                           2009
    *The Entrepreneurial Effect*

3.   Gilles Paquet                                              2009
     *Scheming virtuously: the road to collaborative governance*
2.   Ruth Hubbard                                               2009
     *Profession: Public Servant*
1.   Robin Higham                                               2009
     *Who do we think we are: Canada's reasonable
     (and less reasonable) accommodation debates*

* 9 7 8 0 7 7 6 6 3 8 4 6 1 *